PUNTER

RICKY PONTING
with Peter Staples

PUNTER
First Tests of a Champion

RICKY PONTING
with Peter Staples

IRONBARK
Pan Macmillan Australia

First published 1998 in Ironbark by Pan Macmillan Australia Pty Limited
St Martins Tower, 31 Market Street, Sydney

Copyright © Ricky Ponting 1998

All rights reserved. No part of this book may be reproduced or
transmitted in any form or by any
means, electronic or mechanical, including photocopying,
recording or by any informational
storage and retrieval system, without prior permission in writing
from the publisher.

National Library of Australia
cataloguing-in-publication data:

Ponting Ricky.
Punter: first tests of a champion.

ISBN 0 330 36117 1.

1. Ponting, Ricky. 2. Cricket players—Australia—Biography.
I. Staples, Peter. 1952– . II. Title.

796.358092

Typeset by Midland Typesetters
Printed in Australia by McPherson's Printing Group

CONTENTS

Foreword		vii
Part one	**The Player**	
Introduction		3
Chapter one	**Life before cricket**	7
Chapter two	**Raising a champion**	17
Chapter three	**A rising star**	23
Chapter four	**The journey begins**	27
Chapter five	**Time for Shield cricket**	37
Chapter six	**The first steps**	49
Chapter seven	**A Test berth awaits**	59
Chapter eight	**The World Cup controversy**	75
Chapter nine	**The first season**	91
Chapter ten	**The Ashes tour of England**	111

Part two	The Game	
Chapter eleven	The pressures of an international game	121
Chapter twelve	A professional game	131
Chapter thirteen	Giving something back	139
Chapter fourteen	The trials and tribulations on tour	143
Chapter fifteen	The techniques of a champion	149
Chapter sixteen	The highlights and pitfalls of professional cricket	155
Chapter seventeen	Fun and frivolity on and off the field	169
Chapter eighteen	Ricky looks to the future	175
Chapter nineteen	The statistics of a champion	181

FOREWORD

THERE are few better jobs in world cricket than Head Coach of the Commonwealth Bank Cricket Academy. The reason—well, you get to see the cream of Australia's young cricketers each year. You get to work with them for eight months and then all being equal you get to see them forge a career in first-class, then international cricket.

I have been in the position for almost eight years and as each year draws to an end I look forward to the new year and the Australian Youth Championships each January.

It is at these Under-17 and Under-19 Championships our coaching staff (with the help of the national selectors and the State coaching staffs) search for that extraordinary talent to invite to Adelaide to join the Academy.

As luck would have it, I didn't have to search for Ricky Ponting at these under-age championships. In my first year at the Academy (1991) he was sent on a two-week scholarship by the Century Club in Launceston.

Ricky was just sixteen and it was obvious he oozed talent. People often ask how do you know a kid is going to make it? When you looked at R. Ponting, age 16, you just knew.

It was more than talent, it was an understanding of the game, an awareness of what was required and a determination to listen to and observe the best in action.

A good example of this was Ricky watching Tendulkar train at Adelaide Oval in 1992. He sat and watched the young genius have his net and I reckon everything about his batting was absorbed and computed in those fifteen minutes.

Ricky toured South Africa with the Commonwealth Bank Cricket Academy in 1992 and India and Sri Lanka in 1993. On both trips he impressed astute judges and it was only going to be a matter of time before he broke into the Tasmanian line-up.

Tasmanian Coach Greg Shipperd phoned me non-stop (it seemed) about his progress. He was ready to play and probably had been for a year. Ricky was an instant success and of course the press started ringing.

I had two options. Number one was to play down the class of the young man or number two to tell the truth and say he was the best seventeen-year-old batsman I had ever seen and that all being equal he would play for Australia.

By choosing the second option I knew Ricky would be under enormous pressure but as I said to him 'you will have to absorb this kind of pressure as you make your way to the top so you may as well get used to it now!'

Ricky has handled this pressure very well and one would expect him to become Australia's premium batsmen as we get into the next millennium.

Ricky's talent extends past batting. He fields like a panther, can bowl useful swingers and spinners, and hits a golf ball better than a lot of pros going around. He loves his footy and could have played at the top level had he so desired.

Ricky Ponting

People will always want to watch Ricky play the game as he is an entertainer. Thankfully, we will have this opportunity for some years to come.

Rodney Marsh
September 1998

Part one

The Player

INTRODUCTION

EVEN at the tender age of four Ricky Thomas Ponting was destined to wear the prized 'Baggy Green Cap' and realise his dream of one day playing Test cricket for Australia.

When the little tike from Prospect, a small suburb of the city of Launceston in northern Tasmania, had just turned four, his grandmother, Nana Connie (Ponting), gave him a T-shirt and on it was inscribed 'Inside this shirt is an Australian Test cricketer'.

Call it intuition or pure fluke, for who could know that on that day when Ricky slipped that T-shirt over his head, he *was* destined to achieve every cricketer's dream.

Only days before he celebrated his 21st birthday, Ricky walked onto the WACA oval in Perth for his Test debut against Sri Lanka. And, but for a controversial leg before wicket decision, the latest shining light of Tasmanian cricket may have joined an elite band of cricketing greats who struck a century on their Test debuts.

Ricky's rise to the Test arena and success is the result of dedication and a self belief inspired by family and friends who helped steer him on a course to greatness.

Tagged a batting prodigy in his early teens in Tasmania, he was closely watched and encouraged by some of the nation's most revered Test heroes including former great Australian wicket-keeper Rodney Marsh.

While Ricky is only in the infant stage of his Test and one-day international career, he has made an enormous impact on the international scene since his Test debut and is poised to follow a similar path to that taken by fellow Tasmanian David Boon who, when at his peak, was arguably the best batsman in the world.

When Ricky was only a toddler, a cricket bat was always within arm's reach—an old battered piece of willow took pride of place by his bed.

From the age of eight, Ricky's weekends and school holidays were spent playing many sports, including soccer, golf and Aussie Rules. He had a passion for football during the winter months but as soon as the football was safely tucked away in the cupboard following that last weekend in September, Ricky was out in his backyard wielding his trusty blade.

Like many Test cricketers before him, Ricky and a small band of budding young Bradmans contested mock Tests in the local park. Here Ricky honed the skills with bat and ball which would eventually take him to the pinnacle in his chosen sport.

Unable to play cricket at Mowbray Primary School until grade five, his passion for the game bubbled away inside. Whenever a Test match or one-day international was on television Ricky's eyes were glued to the set along with his parents, Graeme and Lorraine, who also share their son's love of the game.

Ricky unleashed his natural talent in only his second

primary-school game scoring an unbeaten half-century on a sunny spring day in 1985, aged ten. Even then he was the nemesis of his rivals, refusing to hand up his wicket with a rash shot, respecting the good balls and despatching the loose deliveries to the boundary.

His determination to preserve his wicket was a sign of things to come and helped pave the way for his entry onto the greatest cricket stage of all—the Test arena.

This is the story, so far, of a young boy from Tasmania who dreamed of one day being a professional cricketer— and the first tests of a champion.

Chapter one

LIFE BEFORE CRICKET

RICKY Ponting was a quiet, unassuming child of pleasant nature, and affectionately described by his mother as an 'ideal child'.

Most children have teddy bears or some other form of soft cuddly toy when growing up but the two most prized possessions in Ricky's bedroom were a cricket bat and a football.

In his formative years, playing cricket and football were as much a part of Ricky's life as sitting down at the breakfast table each morning to a bowl of Weet-Bix and a glass of orange juice.

Ricky grew up in a sporting environment. His father, Graeme, was a handy grade cricketer and low handicap golfer, and his mother Lorraine was a competitive sportswoman who excelled in vigoro (for which she represented the State), netball and badminton and who also showed prowess on the golf course.

Academically, Ricky was an average student with homework usually taking a back seat to his sporting activities. 'From as far back as I can remember all I ever wanted to do was play sport and everything else came a distant second. I was an average student but I enjoyed school and progressed through primary school without any problems and I did well in my first two years at high school.

'School work was never a problem and there were plenty of subjects I liked but as far back as I can remember the only thing that really mattered to me was my sport. I felt deep down that one day I would make a living from sport and I made that my number one goal in my first year at Brooks High School.'

Ricky showed a commitment to his passion that was unusual in most teenagers. 'I was never bothered with social activities unless it involved cricket or football. I never went to school dances or things like that because I preferred to stay at home and kick a footy or hit a cricket ball until the sun went down and then I'd probably bury my head in a sports book of some kind. Girls didn't really interest me unless they knew how to play cricket or footy!'

At primary school, because of rules regarding sport at Mowbray Primary, Ricky was unable to unleash his natural talent as a cricketer and footballer. 'I played heaps of backyard cricket and park footy but in those days you weren't allowed to play either sport for the school until you hit grade five. It was a stupid rule but there was nothing we could do about it so I had a go at some other sports.'

Naturally athletic, Ricky was an enthusiastic player of sports. 'I played soccer from when I was eight and I can remember running onto the field and kicking the ice off the grass at some ungodly hour of the morning. Even so it was a lot of fun.'

But when Ricky reached the fifth grade and he strolled

to the crease for the first time, any thoughts of making soccer his first choice were quickly banished to the back blocks for all time.

The local park, only a stone's throw from the Pontings' family home at Newnham, was a haven for Ricky and his six or seven chums who spent most Sundays in summer portraying their cricket heroes. In Ricky's case it was former Test captain Kim Hughes. 'I loved the way Kim Hughes played the game. He was a dashing batsman and was brilliant in the field—I guess he was my role model.'

Ricky and his friends had some good times playing out Tests at the local park. They even used a real cricket ball whenever they could. 'We wanted to make it as authentic as possible but when I look back it might have been a bit dangerous because none of us ever wore any kind of protective gear when we batted. We *were* only kids!

'It was a great place to play cricket because there was this big high cross-mesh fence at one end that was used as the boundary. But we still managed to break the odd window when we hooked or pulled a ball. In the end that cost us ... One Sunday we arrived at the park to find a sign saying only tennis balls were allowed to be used when cricket was played in the park.'

Confined to tennis balls Ricky and his fellow lovers of the game still continued to hone their batting skills on a diet of medium pace, off-breaks and a hefty share of full tosses. Hard ball or soft, his practice was going to pay off.

Back to that spring day in 1985, from the moment Ricky despatched a delivery to the square leg boundary in his first innings for Mowbray Primary, everyone watching could see that this pint-sized kid with the collar-length wavy hair possessed above-average ability. His batting technique was raw but his timing was superb and his panther-like speed in the field made Ricky a standout.

Ricky was taught to never do anything in half measures, and it was that upbringing which helped him achieve his ultimate goal. 'Mum and Dad told me to always try and do my best at whatever I was doing. That attitude has helped me reach where I am today.'

Ricky was like a sponge, absorbing everything about the game and he loved to visit the change rooms before the start of district and Shield games.

'Dad took me to heaps of cricket matches and I loved it when he got me into the change rooms. I remember sitting in a corner just listening to what the players were talking about. As they discussed tactics I was oblivious to everything else that was going on around me. I was completely fascinated. The bowlers would discuss how they would try to get a particular batsman out. Later on when I would watch how the captain and bowler placed the field to bring on a dismissal, I was just as excited as the players when it came off.

'I also loved sneaking a look at the different types of cricket gear the players were using. I've always been obsessed with cricket gear and when I was young I probably used to drive some of the senior players crazy with my questions about why they were using a particular brand of bat or what made one style of batting glove better than another.'

Before playing grade cricket Ricky spent most of his Saturdays working the scoreboard at the Northern Tasmania Cricket Association ground in Launceston, enjoying a bird's-eye view of the action.

'I loved working the scoreboard during Sheffield Shield

games because it gave me a better feel for the game and I felt involved.

'Sometimes after a game I would get Dad to bowl to me and I'd try and emulate some of the shots I had seen played that day. I guess it was just a part of the learning process and in the early days my teacher was the game itself. Although Dad showed me the basics. We worked together on improving my batting technique as well as other parts of the game for even back then I loved fielding and wicket-keeping.

'I think sitting in the change rooms when I was just a nipper, listening to and watching what the older guys were doing, helped me enormously but I guess Dad was my first coach and he did a pretty good job. He never pulled any punches when we discussed a bad shot that got me out in a game and he did much the same when I played football. But most importantly he never pushed me into playing any particular sport and it was only when I decided that I wanted help with either my cricket or football that he offered advice.

'Sure, he was hard on me at times but when I look back on it, I wouldn't have wanted it any other way.'

Ian Young was the first person other than his dad who coached Ricky on an one-on-one basis. He was a family friend and Ricky grew up with his son, the very talented cricketer Shaun Young who made his debut for Australia in England in 1997.

'Ian took me to the NTCA ground and set up the bowling machine which was great because it helped me iron out a few problems with my batting technique. I used to love my sessions with Ian. He was a big help with my technique in the early stages of my career.'

When not playing cricket Ricky was on the golf course and his natural hand–eye coordination and exquisite timing ensured he also excelled in that sport. In no time Ricky was playing off a mid-teen handicap and when he turned thirteen he was on the verge of breaking to single figures.

'Most of my mates played golf and we were competitive almost from the outset and in no time at all I had my handicap down to the low teens, but I liked golf because it was an individual's competition. It is the sort of game that can really suck you in—and I was no exception.

'I think golf is one of the greatest games ever invented because you can get out on the course on your own and have a hit, the challenge is between you and that little white ball. The game is a great leveller.'

Football was also one of Ricky's great loves. At one stage he had thoughts of pursuing a career in that sport.

He is an avid fan of AFL club North Melbourne, and North Launceston in the Tasmanian Football League, for which he played at under-age level.

After captaining the northern region grade six primary school team in a statewide competition series he signed on with North Launceston Football Club and he was a dominant player in that club's under-age teams playing mostly in the centre or as a ruck-rover.

'There was a time when I was not sure whether I would pursue a career in football or cricket. I loved my footy.'

But fate chimed in when he was fourteen, playing for his beloved North Launceston in an under-17 game.

Ricky broke the humerus in his right arm when attempting to tackle an opposition player.

'I had to have pins put in the arm and the injury was so

bad that the doctors said I would be out of the game for at least fourteen weeks.

'It finished my football career because I haven't played a game since!'

Many first-class cricketers, including Simon O'Donnell and Shane Warne, were forced to choose between cricket or football, but for Ricky the arm injury removed the option.

'I don't know whether I would ever have made it to the AFL but I never lost any sleep over it. I just regard the injury as a blessing in disguise.

'At one stage I was concerned that the arm injury might also stop me from playing cricket but they did a pretty good job on pinning the bones—and it hasn't bothered me since.'

Ricky suffered another injury in his early teens that could also have ended his sporting career. His mother Lorraine remembers vividly: 'It was VFL Grand Final day and we were all watching the football on television when one of Ricky's mates burst into the house and said Ricky had been hurt in an accident.

'Ricky had been playing cricket and the ball had rolled into a drain and Ricky's mate had lifted a grid on the drain so Rick could retrieve the ball. Unfortunately this kid dropped the iron grid on Ricky's foot.'

Both Lorraine and Graeme rushed off to help their son. They were worried by what they saw.

'Graeme was scared to take Ricky's sock off for fear of seeing some of his toes cut off. Luckily that wasn't the case and the doctors were able to repair the damage.'

At fourteen, Ricky's cricketing career was well under way and as a regular member of Mowbray's A-grade team he quickly came to grips with playing with older cricketers.

'I had always played out of my age group in competition and to be honest I never thought too much about playing with and against the men. If anything, it helped me enormously because I learned at a very early age what was required to play the game at the top level.'

The most memorable moment in Ricky's first season of A-grade cricket occurred in his debut game.

'I was fielding in the gully against Launceston and Richard Bennett was batting and he cut a ball off Troy Cooley. The ball flew off his bat like a rocket. I dived to my right and snapped up the catch low down.

'I can remember our wicket-keeper Richard Soule, who also was the State keeper, ran over to me. He said it was one of the best catches he had ever seen. Knowing he was a State cricketer with a good reputation, his comments made me feel pretty special.'

While Ricky's introduction into top-level cricket was based on his prowess with the bat, he never made it to the crease in that match. However, Mowbray won the contest with Ricky's catch hailed as a major turning point in the game.

'I guess I've taken hundreds of catches over the years but that one in my first game with Mowbray is stuck in the memory bank forever.'

Ricky's catch made the headlines of the local newspaper and by this stage the name Ricky Ponting was being bandied about as a future player for Tasmania.

Ricky began to seriously contemplate his cricketing future towards the end of his fourth year at Brooks High School.

'Just before I left school, when I was fifteen, my schoolmates asked me what I was going to do with my life and I told them I was going to play cricket. A lot of them laughed and said I was a dill but I was determined to make it happen.

'Initially, I went to work at Scotch Oakburn College as a groundsman, but four months later I was inducted into the AIS Cricket Academy. It was starting to happen.'

Chapter two

RAISING A CHAMPION

RICKY, twenty-three, is the eldest of three children born to Lorraine and Graeme Ponting. Ricky's brother Drew is two years his junior and sister Renee, seventeen, is the baby of the family.

Like Ricky, Drew and Renee are keen on sport and both excel at golf with Drew already identified as a future star having made the State junior golf team and earned a scholarship with the Tasmanian Institute of Sport.

Graeme admits to being a typical Aussie battler and Lorraine shares those sentiments.

Raising a happy and healthy family was their priority. Graeme says he had no hesitation in giving up a career as a professional golfer to ensure he could be a decent provider for his family. This has meant taking on a variety of jobs including his present position as groundsman at Oakburn Scotch College in Launceston.

Graeme and Lorraine were always aware of their eldest son's talent and Graeme has fond memories of what it was like watching his son develop into one of the best cricketers Tasmania has ever produced.

'Ricky was a cricket fanatic when he was four or five and you could see he had a passion for the game way back then. As soon as the cricket season started he was out in the backyard or down at the park with his bat, ball and set of stumps and, more often than not, it was Mum and Dad who had the job of bowling to him!

'He was a terrific kid who just loved his cricket and football, and I guess he was the type of child every parent dreams of having.'

Ricky was rarely chastised but there was one occasion which warranted some stern action.

'Ricky was very late home from school one afternoon and we were on the verge of sending out a search party when he strolled in through the back door,' Graeme says. 'When asked where he had been Ricky told us he had been at his mate Nathan Jameson's place doing some homework—that in itself was a dead giveaway that the boys had been up to something else! I noticed Ricky's shoes were left outside the back door and when I checked I noticed they were wet and mud-stained.

'I confronted Ricky about the mud on his shoes and he confessed to sneaking off to the golf club and wading through the creek looking for golf balls.

'He copped a hiding for telling lies but that was the only time he ever felt my wrath. It taught him a lesson not to tell lies but giving him that whack on the backside hurt me as much as it did him—I was a blithering mess afterwards.'

The incident did nothing to alter Ricky's love and affection for his father and the bond between them continued to grow, especially when it came to sport.

Graeme had hoped to one day play in a team with his teenage son and in 1987 Ricky was selected to play for

Mowbray thirds of which Graeme was captain.

'I can remember the day I walked to the crease with my son at the other end in a match against South Launceston on our home ground like it was yesterday. It was a magic feeling. However, the end result didn't quite pan out as I had imagined. When I got to the crease Ricky strolled over and told me the leg-spinner, Matthew Dillon, who was bowling at the time, was doing a bit with the ball and that I should just watch the first couple of deliveries.

'But I had other ideas. I took a swipe at the second ball I faced and skied it to cover and was caught! When I looked up at Ricky he was just standing at the other end, shaking his head in disbelief.'

However, father and son managed to share a couple of enterprising partnerships before the season ended.

'It was terrific just watching Ricky grow in stature and there was one game which made me realise the impact Ricky was making on the sport,' Graeme says. 'It was in a match against Riverside and Ricky, who was only thirteen, looked set for a big innings and the opposition captain Troy Walters set a trap for Ricky, by moving a man in close on the leg side. The move resulted in Ricky's dismissal for when he tried to turn one off his pads, the ball found a leading edge which went straight to the close-in fieldsman. But I was proud of him that day because he had earned the respect of the opposition captain.'

Ricky also relished playing in the same team as his dad. 'It was a terrific feeling strolling out onto the field with Dad and I'm sure our relationship became stronger because a father and son don't often get the opportunity to play together in a team sport.'

Graeme played out the season but opted to give the game

away and concentrate on his first love—golf.

'Ricky moved to A-grade the following season and I felt I had gone as far as I could with the game so it was back to the golf course for me on Saturday afternoons. But Lorraine and I still went to watch Ricky play in some A-grade matches and whenever he played in regional junior competition.'

Lorraine Ponting is a typically proud mother who has fond memories of her eldest child's rise to star status, but being the mum of a Test cricketer can be a nerve-racking experience. She described watching Ricky's first innings for Australia as one of the most traumatic experiences of her life.

'It is very hard to describe the feeling when your son walks onto the ground to play his first Test and when Ricky went in to bat it was like sitting on a knife's edge,' she says. 'From the first ball, which he edged and almost carried to first slip, it was like being out there myself.

'What made it more difficult was the media—there were journalists and TV cameras around us most of the time. Even though we felt a bit uncomfortable, we understood that it was just part and parcel of how things are today with sport and the media.

'There were times during his innings that I felt like pinching myself just to make sure it was real because for so long it had been Rick's dream to play Test cricket.

'When he reached his 50 and he raised his bat to me I didn't know whether to jump up and scream or just burst into tears—I think I did both.

'Then things became very tense when he reached 80 and the media started to close in. They seemed more interested in our reactions than Ricky's.'

As Ricky made his way to 96 there was great expectation that the young gun from Tasmania would emulate the feat of one of Australia's cricketing heroes, Doug Walters, and blaze a ton on debut.

But it was not to be and the disappointment of Ricky being given out leg before wicket in controversial circumstances left Lorraine with very mixed emotions.

'When he was given out I was disappointed for Ricky. Everyone around us thought it was a tough call.

'And what was really deflating was being right next to the media and when Ricky was given out, they were gone in a flash. It was like someone had opened up a hole in the ground and we all just fell in.

'But it was my most proudest moment when he walked out to bat and it wouldn't have mattered had Ricky made a duck, because he had worked hard to achieve his goal. I was just so proud to be his mum.

'I said then that I didn't care if I never saw him play another Test because I was there at his first one and that's the one that counts most.'

Whenever Ricky is playing for Australia outside of Tasmania, Lorraine is either glued to a television set or has an ear stuck to the radio. 'Sometimes I wonder why I watch the Test and one-day matches on television because I become so engrossed it's like I play every shot and field every ball. However, I've spoken to parents of other players and they all tell me it's the same for them.'

Lorraine was always confident Ricky would achieve his ultimate goal. 'Ricky was always very quiet as a child who wouldn't say boo to a goose and in a way he still has that disposition. But he was very determined to do well in most things he tackled, especially sport. He was a natural ball player and probably could have carved a career in golf, football or even soccer, had he set his mind to it, but in the end he chose cricket.'

Lorraine's brother is Greg Campbell who played for Tasmania and momentarily for Australia in the 1980s. He also was an encouraging influence on the young Ricky Ponting.

'Every time Greg came home he would be out in the backyard with Rick and they would play for hours,' Lorraine remembers. 'Greg was a good cricketer and I think his success was an inspiration to Rick but we would not have known that for sure because Rick has always been one to keep his feelings to himself. Once he came home from cricket and I asked him what sort of a day he had had and he gave his usual one-word reply—okay. Then he went into his room to put his gear away and came back out and sat down for dinner. This time I asked how he went and he casually told me he made 150! Then he asked me to pass the salt and pepper, and that was the end of the conversation. That was Rick. He never bragged about any of his achievements then and he is much the same today.'

Chapter three

A RISING STAR

RICKY'S determination to do well at sport was evident from an early age, but while playing for Australia was a dream, it was not something on which he specifically set his sights as a primary-school kid.

'Every kid who loves the game, like I did, wants to play Test cricket for Australia, but it was not a conscious goal of mine until I was well into my teens.

'My first real goal was to represent the Northern region in the under-13 schoolboys carnival and I achieved that because it was achievable.

'I never saw it as setting goals back then. It was just something I wanted to do and I worked as hard as I could to make it happen.'

Ricky's performances during the 1986 under-13 regional carnival earned him star status. He compiled four successive centuries, three of which were unbeaten, and those efforts earned him promotion into the Northern under-16 XI the following week.

'I don't remember a lot about the four centuries I hit in the under-13 competition but I felt pretty good about the ton I reached when promoted to the under-16 team in the final week of the carnival.

'When I was playing in the under-13 competition I was hoping to be bumped up to the under-16s, so that was another goal I achieved.

'Every time I went out to bat I wanted to make a century so that was a constant goal but there were times when I got out to a stupid shot and the feeling I had then is much the same as it is today when I get dismissed without having made a decent contribution to the team score.'

Ricky was rewarded for his performances during the under-age carnival when cricket equipment manufacturer Kookaburra came on the scene. The southern regional sales manager of Kookaburra, Ian Simpson, was in Tasmania for the Kookaburra Cup competition and Ian Young, Ricky's 'coach' and family friend of the Pontings, set up a meeting. Soon Ricky Ponting had a sponsorship deal.

'The meeting went well and Kookaburra agreed to sign me up and supply me with new gear. I was a fanatic about cricket gear. I can remember the first night I got my gear from Kookaburra. I set it up on the lounge at home and just sat there admiring it!

'It was an awesome feeling. I don't think I did anything else that night except look at all that brilliant new gear.

'At that stage I was the youngest person to receive a sponsorship deal from Kookaburra. Apparently the big boss wasn't too enthused about signing on an unknown young kid just out of primary school, but the deal went ahead anyway. I've been with the company ever since.'

It was while admiring his new Kookaburra equipment that Ricky realised for the first time he might have a big future in the game and he began to contemplate his future.

'Getting all this new gear was a bit special and it was probably then that I realised there were some important people out there who thought I was good at the game and it gave me a bit more confidence.'

Now Ricky Ponting had a new goal—to play regular A-grade cricket for Mowbray and some day Tasmania.

Keeping a level head

Ricky's goals were achieved. Before long he was playing A-grade cricket for Mowbray and then, soon after, Shield cricket. The sponsorship deal, coupled with his performances in schoolboys and grade competition for Mowbray, had the potential to give any young player an inflated opinion of himself, but not Ricky. There were plenty of friends and team-mates around to ensure he did not have a swollen head for any great length of time.

'When I first started playing A-grade with Mowbray there were a lot of players at the club who had played and were still playing Shield cricket like Richard Soule, Troy Cooley, Roger Brown and Brad Jones, and all those blokes told me that if I ever went away and did all right for myself and I came back with a big head they would soon deflate it for me,' Ricky laughs. 'They meant it in the nicest possible way and it was good to know that I had plenty of people around me helping to keep my feet firmly on the ground.'

Ricky's affection for the Mowbray club and its senior players when he first started to make his mark on the game remains intact.

'I thought of playing for Australia like all kids do, but I can vividly remember when all I really wanted was to play regular A-grade cricket for Mowbray and then some day be selected in a Tasmanian under-age team,' Ricky says. 'Club cricket is where it all started for me and a special mateship and bond exists in that scene. Even though I am now playing at the ultimate level and representing my country, sometimes I miss club cricket dreadfully. Whenever I get the rare chance to slip back into club competition I take it and love every minute.'

Chapter four

THE JOURNEY BEGINS

IN early 1991 Ricky spent two weeks at the AIS Cricket Academy in South Australia, courtesy of a sponsorship through the Century Club in Launceston. Suddenly the notion of playing for Australia hit home.

'I went to the AIS with another top junior from Launceston, Andy Gower, and it was at a time when the Australian under-19 team was playing in England and there weren't too many guys left at the Academy. I was lucky to be there at that time and I was determined to make the most of it.

'Spending two weeks training with the best young cricketers in Australia really gave me a taste of what it would be like being a professional cricketer. Just waking up every morning with the knowledge that all I would be doing for the rest of the day was play cricket was the ultimate feeling. And when I had just about finished my fortnight stint at the AIS it dawned on me that if I really applied myself, playing for Australia was a distinct possibility.'

It was former Test star Rodney Marsh's first year as head

coach at the Academy and Ricky made quite an impression on the man. He was to have a big influence on Ricky's career.

Ricky's potential had been acknowledged by the Tasmanian Cricket Association prior to his first visit to the Academy, but it was the reverberation from his fortnight stint in Adelaide which signalled Ricky's arrival as a genuine star of the future destined to play Shield and Test cricket.

In that same year Ricky was awarded a two-year scholarship to attend the Academy. This was a major turning point in his career.

'I was fortunate in being at the Academy at a time when Rod Marsh was coach. He is the ideal bloke to have in charge of the Academy because he is easy to talk to, is a great character but, most of all, he knows a hell of a lot about the game. He is hard but fair and knows how to handle teenagers, and in a way he acts like your away-from-home father.'

It took Ricky a few weeks to settle into full-time Academy lifestyle and it wasn't long before he witnessed Marsh's method of discipline.

'Rod had a rule that if anyone was late for training they were penalised by having to wash cars for a day. While I never had to do it, there were a couple of blokes who learned how to get a nice polish on a car bonnet or two. Another time we were all expected to be at training at the university gym by 8.00 am but a couple of the lads were dragging the chain and the buses were running a bit behind time as well.

'We arrived at the gym about fifteen minutes late and Rod was already there waiting. For the next two weeks we had to start training at 6.00 am.

'In a way it was like being in the army but it taught us

discipline which was obviously one of the reasons behind it. They say the harder you work, the luckier you get. I reckon every bloke at the AIS during my time should have had a fair amount of luck go their way!'

In his first year at the Academy, Ricky earned the princely sum of $40 a month, hardly enough to ensure a decent night out once a week. So he, like many of the other scholarship holders, earned extra money on Sunday mornings by offering their services as specialist coaches for primary-school students.

'Rod suggested we try and earn some extra cash by coaching kids on an one-on-one basis on Sunday mornings. We could earn about $10 an hour and it helped bolster the kitty so we could at least go out on the town once a month. Plus some of the guys needed the extra cash, big time, when they fell foul of Marshy's law—there were varying penalties for playing up, but the one that hurt the most was having your monthly allowance docked.'

Ricky was speaking from experience. It had only happened once but once was enough. And it was his affinity with greyhound racing which led to his allowance loss.

As Ricky tells it: 'A few of the boys decided to go down to the local pub and watch the dog races one Thursday night. After backing a few winners we bought some beers and gave it a nudge.

'When we returned to the units we were staying in, I ended up in the wrong room and woke up late. I had to race off to shower and get ready for the day's training. The problem was I had vomited in the strange bed I had slept in and didn't clean up the mess.

'I got into a bit of strife and it cost me that month's allowance. Mind you, nothing like that ever happened again.'

Ricky also did some football coaching during those years in South Australia—a more reliable way to earn some extra dollars.

During the winter months of 1992 Ricky coached the grades 4–5 Pembroke School Aussie Rules football team.

'I really enjoyed coaching footy and the students from Pembroke were a terrific bunch of kids. I looked forward to Tuesday and Thursday nights getting on my pushbike and riding out to the school. By the end of the season they weren't a bad side.'

One of the children Ricky coached at Pembroke, Simon Callaghan, became an avid follower of cricket as well as a Ponting fan. Christmas from 1991–94 in the Ponting household would not have been the same without a card and a letter from the youngster from South Australia.

'Simon was a terrific kid who would talk to me for ages about cricket and when he played his first game he sent me a letter containing a running description of how he performed. I thought it was great that a kid would go to so much trouble.'

Simon Callaghan was one of many children who idolised Ricky not only for his cricketing prowess but for his willingness to help them develop their skills.

As Ricky says: 'I like working with kids. Sometimes I can see a bit of me in them, but I also really like helping them develop their skills. It is a way of giving back a bit of what the sport has given me.'

The first overseas trip

Ricky made great progress in his first year at the Academy and was subsequently selected in a 13-man Australian youth squad to tour South Africa. It was the first cricket team to make an official visit to the country since Bill Lawry's Australians toured in 1970. This was to, unofficially, launch his international career.

The four-week tour comprised eight matches of which half were limited-over contests. 'At the start of the year I knew there was a South Africa tour on the agenda and I was desperate to be a part of it and I was over the moon when told of my selection,' Ricky says. 'I knew this was my chance to make a big impression and it was a very good squad which included Adam Gilchrist, who was captain, Glenn McGrath, Paul Wilson, Darren Webber and my Tasmanian team-mate Andrew Dykes. It was Rod Marsh's first overseas assignment as coach of an AIS squad and there was an air of expectancy at ACB board level for the team to do well.

'It dawned on me when I was being fitted for my travelling uniform that I was about to represent my country. When that hit home it was a very proud moment in my life. Even though it was not a real representative tour it felt like it to me.'

Most of the team members assembled at Sydney Airport for departure on Qantas flight QF63 and Ricky could envisage for the first time what life would be like as an Australian Test cricketer.

'It wasn't until we all gathered at the airport that I got the real rush of excitement because there I was, this sixteen-year-old kid about to take off and play cricket in a strange country, and from what we had been told it would be in conditions like we had never experienced before,' he says. 'We were all excited with the prospect of taking on the South Africans and we had been told about the wickets being bouncy and fast, similar to the WACA strip in Perth.'

The plane trip passed almost without notice. They had to stop at Perth, Western Australia, to take on the remainder of the squad and then had a ten-hour flight ahead. But it seemed no sooner had the rest of the team boarded the aircraft than they were touching down at Jan Smuts Airport and being ushered into coaches to take them to their hotel in Johannesburg.

The team settled in and all the players were keen to journey to the Wanderers Oval for the first full-scale practice session. As Ricky remembers: 'The first training session was tough and a few players suffered from breathlessness caused by the high altitude, but we soon came to terms with it.'

The first game was scheduled to start on March 11 and the players were champing at the bit to take on a Northern Transvaal XI in Pretoria.

The 1991–92 youth squad's tour was at a time when South Africa was on the verge of entering a new era in the country's history.

Nelson Mandela was a prominent statesman at the time calling for an end to apartheid and decades of political unrest, something of which Ricky and most of the touring party had little knowledge before. Ricky took an interest in the political situation in South Africa and a visit to the black township of Soweto on the eve of the team's first match left an immovable imprint on the teenager.

'I had heard a lot about the way of life in South Africa but nothing I had been told beforehand could have prepared me for what we encountered. Johannesburg is a big city but what amazed me was the difference between life in the city and that of the black townships. There we were in a plush hotel with all the mod cons but about fifteen minutes out of the city were these townships that looked like ghettos.

'I found it difficult to come to terms with the segregation and we all were amazed at the enthusiasm shown by the black children when we visited some of the towns to run coaching clinics. We held one clinic in Soweto, the largest black township in South Africa, with about thirty black kids aged between fifteen and seventeen. I was amazed at the skill level of these kids. They could all probably be Test cricketers if they had access to the AIS Academy like us.'

When the squad held the coaching clinic in Soweto it was exactly one week prior to the Referendum for which every non-white South African and most whites would vote 'Yes'—against apartheid.

'Everywhere we went the main topic of conversation was the Referendum and it was obvious that the outcome of the vote would have a huge bearing on the future of cricket in South Africa, but more so the country's future.

'We were told that if by some chance the Referendum returned a majority No-vote, then we would be despatched back to Australia on the first available flight. Thankfully for all concerned that wasn't the case.'

The prime focus for the youth squad was its opening match against Northern Transvaal on the Centurion Park oval which was the most modern first-class stadium in the country.

'We won the first match and by over 100 runs. Then we turned our attention to a three-day match against a Transvaal under-23 XI at the famous Wanderers Cricket Stadium in Johannesburg.

'All the guys were pretty keyed up about playing at Wanderers and for me it was a big challenge because, apart from a few A-grade games with Mowbray, up until then I had really only played against my own age group.'

The AIS won the toss and batted with Ricky down to bat at number seven. Unfortunately the team's bowling star, Glenn McGrath, was named to carry the drinks owing to a niggling leg injury he suffered in the one-day game against North Transvaal. As Ricky remembers: 'We got off to a shaky start losing openers Ashley Hammond and Anthony McGuire and first drop Andrew Dykes with only 30-odd runs on the board. Luckily Adam Gilchrist and Darren Webber shared a terrific partnership of almost 100 to put some respectability into the score.'

When Ricky walked to the crease the score was 5 for 175 and he was determined to carry his bat through the innings. 'I started slowly and, as always, getting that first run was a big relief. The wicket was a lot faster than I imagined. Even with the shine off the ball it still whipped through quick.'

The AIS innings closed at 241 with Ricky unbeaten on 34 after ninety-nine minutes. His tally included four boundaries. Transvaal replied with eight declared for 296. Ricky was determined to better his first innings tally.

'I made 65 in the second innings and I was fairly pleased with that because I spent about three hours at the crease and helped build a reasonable total for the South Africans to chase.'

The match was drawn but for Ricky it was a satisfying start to the tour.

In the one-day match which followed against an Orange Free State XI, Ricky's contribution was 25 in an 189 total with the AIS emerging victors by 93 runs.

The team finished the tour unbeaten with five wins and three matches drawn.

Ricky ended the tour with a batting average of 45.67, second only to Darren Webber who bettered with his 50. Surprisingly Ricky also topped the bowling averages at 14.33 after taking three wickets from 14 overs at a cost of 43 runs.

'Topping the bowling averages was a bit of a laugh. I must admit I enjoyed rolling the arm over and I got a few of the off-breaks to really cut.

'My top score was 70 in the opening game against North Transvaal but I batted consistently without reaching a really big score.

'When I look back on my career in years to come, the South African tour with the youth squad will always be regarded as one of the greatest stepping stones in my career.'

At the end of the tour, team manager John Edwards delivered his report and as a footnote heaped praise on some individual players of which Ricky was one. As Edwards said of Ricky: 'It is not for me to place my views on record concerning individuals but I do think that Ricky Ponting is as good a player as David Boon was at the same age.'

Chapter five

TIME FOR SHIELD CRICKET

WHEN Ricky returned from the South African tour he set his sights on playing Shield cricket for Tasmania. In November that year, at the Adelaide Oval against South Australia, his goal was realised.

Rod Marsh was pushing for Ricky's inclusion in Tasmania's Shield team and went on record as saying Ricky was the best seventeen-year-old batsmen he had seen. He rated him in the same league as India's batting sensation Sachin Tendulkar.

As Ricky remembers: 'I knew Marshy had given me a big rap and that he was keen to see me play Shield cricket. But in the end it was up to the State selectors and unfortunately they told me I wasn't going to be rushed into the side.

'I was happy with my efforts in South Africa and I was doing well at the Academy so I was really starting to think seriously about playing Shield cricket.

'The media was right behind me and Greg Shipperd was pushing for my inclusion in the Shield team. I also made 161 not out for the AIS against a South Australian Second

XI a month before the first Shield game of the season against SA.'

Ricky was playing well. He also scored a well crafted 168 not out for the AIS against a Queensland Second XI at the 'Gabba in Brisbane a week prior to the game against South Australia. In the Brisbane game he belted twenty-three boundaries and one almighty six over the long-on boundary. It was described as one of the best innings on the 'Gabba by a teenager in decades.

'I was very happy with my pre-season form and I felt that I was ready to make the step up to Shield. And I was particularly pleased to knock up a century for my home club Mowbray.'

In this particular game Ricky belted 114 not out in an unbeaten partnership of 238 with his club skipper and the State wicket-keeper Richard Soule (118 no) to give Mowbray a comfortable victory over arch rival Riverside.

Rod Marsh was determined to give the Tasmanian selectors plenty to think about. He said that while it was not his place to make comments concerning who should and shouldn't be in the Tasmanian side, he believed Ricky's performances on the Adelaide Oval only a month prior to the first Shield match should be enough to give him a berth.

Marsh also suggested Ricky would be able to handle the pressure of moving up to the next level. He said: 'Ricky has made up his mind that he wants to play for Australia and he's certainly going the right way about achieving that. The next hurdle is how well he handles the added pressure of first-class cricket. He has cleared every hurdle so far and I think he could clear the hurdle of first-class cricket if it had barbed wire on top and still have room to spare!'

Ricky was well aware of Marsh's comments but he took it in his stride. He wasn't prepared to count his chickens before they were hatched.

Finally Ricky was selected in the Shield team. 'They were right about the hidden pressures of first-class cricket because I felt it as soon as I walked to the crease. But having David Boon there with me was a big help.'

Ricky scored 56 and shared a brilliant 127-run third-wicket stand with Boon (60) which lasted 142 minutes. Boon said he only had to give Ricky a little encouragement along the way.

While it was not a spectacular start to his first-class career it was a substantial step towards the ultimate goal.

It took Ricky 13 balls to break his duck but then he unveiled an array of shots more befitting a seasoned first-class veteran than a seventeen-year-old kid fresh out of the AIS Cricket Academy.

Ricky rewrote the record books when he walked out onto the Adelaide Oval becoming the youngest person to play Shield cricket for Tasmania at seventeen years, 337 days, reducing by 14 days the previous record held by David Boon. As he says: 'I have never been one for records and trivia but it was a bit special knowing I was the youngest to play Shield cricket for Tassie and to take over the mantle from Boonie. He was an inspiration to me when I was growing up and seeing him do so well and making a big name for himself at Test level gave me something to which I could aspire. The third-wicket partnership of 127 I shared with him on my debut and having him out in the middle with me made a hell of a difference to my confidence.

'We were struggling a bit at 2 for 50 when I went in to bat and Boonie and I set about building the total. I got

Punter—First Tests of a Champion

SOUTH AUSTRALIA v TASMANIA
Adelaide Oval, Adelaide. November 20, 21, 22, 23, 1992
Toss: South Australia. Result: South Australia won by 215 runs

SOUTH AUSTRALIA

FIRST INNINGS	RUNS	SECOND INNINGS	RUNS
GS Blewett c Tucker b Young	23	c Courtney b Matthews	43
NR Fielke c Courtney b Matthews	6	st Atkinson b Boon	74
JA Brayshaw c Hills b Young	23	not out	73
JD Siddons c Hills b Young	25	not out	69
GA Bishop b Miller	50		
TJ Nielsen c McPhee b Tucker	109		
JC Scuderi not out	100		
PR Sleep c Matthews b Tucker	13		
TBA May not out	3		
DA Reeves			
DJ Hickey			
Sundries (B 1, LB 9, NB 12)	16	(B 1, LB 5, W 1, NB 4)	9
TOTAL (Overs: 130.0—Mins: 497)	7 dec 368	(Overs: 65.0—Mins: 223)	2 dec 268

F/W 9 60 61 108 168 327 359

120 124

Bowler	Ovrs	Mdns	Runs	Wkts	NB	W
FIRST INNINGS						
Matthews	25	4	76	1	2	—
McPhee	28	5	87	—	4	—
Miller	32	8	90	1	—	—
Young	27	9	50	3	—	—
Tucker	17	1	54	2	—	—
Boon	1	—	1	—	—	—
SECOND INNINGS						
Matthews	15	2	64	1	—	1
McPhee	14	2	60	—	—	—
Miller	9	1	46	—	—	—
Young	5	3	2	—	—	—
Boon	15	3	56	1	—	—
Courtney	7	—	34	—	2	—

TASMANIA

FIRST INNINGS	RUNS	SECOND INNINGS	RUNS
DF Hills lbw Reeves	16	lbw May	20
NCP Courtney c Bishop b Hickey	16	b May	43
DC Boon* c Sleep b May	60	c Nielsen b Reeves	8
RT Ponting c Nielsen b Hickey	56	b Hickey	4
J Cox c May b Hickey	11	lbw Scuderi	18
RJ Tucker not out	49	c Siddons b Reeves	6
S Young c Siddons b May	0	c & b May	7
CD Matthews not out	29	b Sleep	4
MN Atkinson†		c Siddons b May	1
CR Miller		not out	0
PT McPhee		c Fielke b May	0
Sundries (LB 6, W 10, NB 90)	61	(LB 3, W 3, NB 12)	12
TOTAL (Overs: 89.0—Mins: 332)	6 dec 298	(Overs: 76.4—Mins: 269)	123

F/W 31 50 177 195 213 216

27 40 46 87 96 105 122 122 123 123

Bowler	Ovrs	Mdns	Runs	Wkts	NB	W
FIRST INNINGS						
Hickey	18	4	75	3	12	8
Reeves	15	1	60	1	—	2
Scuderi	10	—	44	—	12	—
May	35	9	80	2	20	—
Blewett	1	1	0	—	—	—
Sleep	10	—	33	—	—	—
SECOND INNINGS						
Hickey	14	1	37	1	—	3
Reeves	13	5	27	2	—	—
May	32.4	15	42	5	6	—
Sleep	8	5	3	1	—	—
Scuderi	9	5	11	1	—	—

Umpires: SJ Davis, DJ Harper
12th Men: DS Webber (South Australia) & MG Farrell (Tasmania)

56 which I suppose wasn't a bad effort on debut although it would have been better had I cracked a ton.'

It wasn't long before Ricky was making headlines at Shield level and in his seventh Shield game against NSW at the SCG in January 1993, he took another step up the staircase to national selection.

Making centuries was nothing new to Ricky but this well-crafted ton again had the statisticians etching his name in the record books.

His 125, against a strong Blues attack, made him the youngest Tasmanian, at age eighteen years and forty days, to score a first-class century, overshadowing the previous record held by Jack Badcock who was eighteen years and 261 days when he scored 100 against Victoria in Hobart during the 1933–34 season.

Ricky also became the fifth youngest Australian to score

NEW SOUTH WALES v TASMANIA
Sydney Cricket Ground, Sydney. January 27, 28, 29, 30, 1993
Toss: Tasmania. Result: Match Drawn

TASMANIA

FIRST INNINGS	RUNS	SECOND INNINGS	RUNS
DF Hills c Matthews b McGrath	3	c Freedman b Matthews	101
NCP Courtney c Bevan b McGrath	20	c Small b Matthews	8
J Cox lbw Matthews	33	c Slater b Freedman	1
RT Ponting c Small b Holdsworth	125	c Small b Matthews	69
DJ Buckingham c McNamara b Matthews	29	lbw McNamara	18
RJ Tucker* c Emery b Holdsworth	3	c Small b McNamara	3
CD Matthews c Emery b Matthews	0	(10) not out	18
S Young c McNamara b McGrath	23	(7) run out	18
MG Farrell lbw McGrath	17	(8) c McNamara b Matthews	3
MN Atkinson† c Matthews b McGrath	23	(9) lbw Matthews	46
PT McPhee not out	1	not out	0
Sundries (B 1, LB 5, W 1, NB 16)	15	(LB 7, W 1, NB 4)	10
TOTAL (Overs: 121.1—Mins: 455)	292	(Overs: 139.0—Mins: 474) 9 for	295

F/W 11 35 107 191 196 197 246 257 287 292

45 50 159 192 204 205 210 264 283

Bowler	Ovrs	Mdns	Runs	Wkts	NB	W
FIRST INNINGS						
Holdsworth	23	5	74	2	4	1
McGrath	29.1	9	79	5	2	—
McNamara	9	3	14	—	—	—
Matthews	46	15	78	3	—	—
Freedman	14	5	41	—	2	—
SECOND INNINGS						
Holdsworth	17	4	41	—	—	—
McGrath	13.3	6	29	—	—	—
Matthews	54	31	61	5	—	1
Freedman	22	3	80	1	—	—
Bayliss	10	4	29	—	—	—
Bevan	9	1	25	—	—	—
McNamara	13.3	4	23	2	2	—

NEW SOUTH WALES

FIRST INNINGS	RUNS
SM Small b Matthews	0
MJ Slater c Atkinson b Matthews	79
TH Bayliss c Atkinson b Matthews	0
MG Bevan c Tucker b McPhee	76
GRJ Matthews c Atkinson b Matthews	18
BE McNamara c Buckingham b Farrell	51
AC Gilchrist lbw Young	16
PA Emery*† not out	47
DA Freedman c Atkinson b Farrell	12
WJ Holdsworth c Ponting b Tucker	17
GD McGrath	
Sundries (B 4, LB 8, W 4, NB 12)	22
TOTAL (Overs: 121.2—Mins: 469) 9 dec	338

F/W 0 0 153 176 188 213 284 316 338

Bowler	Ovrs	Mdns	Runs	Wkts	NB	W
FIRST INNINGS						
Matthews	32	10	80	4	—	3
McPhee	25	7	83	1	6	—
Young	23	11	42	1	—	1
Tucker	18.2	5	53	1	—	—
Farrell	23	5	68	2	—	—

Umpires: PE Dodd, IG Jackson
12th Men: S Lee (New South Wales) & TJ Cooley (Tasmania)

a first-class century behind only Ian Craig, Archie Jackson, Doug Walters and Clem Hill.

'My first Shield century was a nerve-racking experience because I was 98 at the end of the day's play and I had to sleep on that score,' he says. 'I felt all right about it until it was time to go to bed and I started thinking about some of the shots I might play to reach the ton.

'I had a dream that I was run out going for a quick single to bring up the century! Strangely I still have that dream occasionally.'

Ricky made 69 in the second innings, a rewarding match for him as an individual player, but Tasmania lost, which dulled his sense of achievement.

In the second-last match of the season against Western Australia in Perth, Ricky finally strung together two top-class knocks. 'I set a goal of making 500 runs in my first Shield season and I made 643 so it wasn't a bad effort and I was most pleased about scoring a century in both innings of the Shield game against WA at Bellerive.'

Ricky scored 107 in the first innings and notched an unbeaten 100 on his return to the crease. His first full season of first-class cricket was rewarding.

'I would rather have finished the season on a better note because I only got a handful in both innings against

Queensland at Bellerive. But I finished with an average of 46 which wasn't too bad.'

Ricky notched three centuries in Shield competition the following season which culminated in his 161 against South Australia on the Adelaide Oval. This was his best and helped Tasmania make it into its first Shield final.

'My second season of Shield started well with a century against WA at Bellerive but then my form started to slip. I got a start in most games but I was getting out to silly shots. It was probably one of the most frustrating times in my career.

'It wasn't until the return match against WA that I put it all together and scored 101 and that century was, in my mind, better than the first of the season.

'I followed up with 84 not out and 161 in the second innings against South Australia which helped get us into our first Shield final. That was one of my most satisfying innings.

'However, I failed in the final against NSW at the SCG and that must be one of my most disappointing experiences in first-class cricket.'

At the end of his second Shield season Ricky boasted a batting average of 47.22 and was being touted as a future Test player.

The 1994–95 Shield season promised to be his best and a brilliant 119 at the 'Gabba against Queensland against a strong bowling line-up in the season opener was just the start he was looking for. Ricky knew that some big scores early in the season would enhance his chances of claiming a berth in the Australian team for the West Indies tour.

'It was a great start to the season but I didn't back it up in the second innings scoring in the low thirties. And a 45 and 16 wasn't what I was hoping for in the next match against SA in Adelaide.'

But his performance in the following game against WA at Bellerive proved to be the launching pad of his international career.

When he strolled to the crease on a placid Bellerive strip it was evident from the outset that a big score was in the offing. 211 runs later Ricky was the toast of Tasmania and in registering his highest first-class score he equalled Sir Donald Bradman's record of six successive centuries against WA in Sheffield Shield matches.

'From the first shot that day I felt "in the zone" and there have been few times since that I felt that good. It was a chanceless double century that made it even more pleasing and it was against a very strong attack that included Bruce Reid, Brendan Julien, Jamie Stewart and Tom Moody.

'The team needed a big score and the partnership of well over 300 I shared with Rod Tucker would have to be one of the most memorable in my career.

'From a personal point of view I knew that it would have made an impression on the national selectors and two weeks later I was selected in an Australian XI to play against an England XI at Bellerive and I scored 71 in that match.

'I scored another century [134] against NSW at Bellerive that season and I was rewarded in the end.'

In three Shield seasons Ricky had taken giant steps towards realising his ultimate goal. At the end of his first Shield season in 1992–93 his batting average was 46 and by the end of the 1994–95 season he had stretched that to 51.41. His third season was by far his best and most consistent and his highest first-class score of 211 against Western Australia at Bellerive in November 1994 is one knock he will never forget.

At the end of the 1997–98 season Ricky's Sheffield Shield tally was 3860 runs for an average of 61.27 derived from 40 matches and 73 innings. Simply astounding!

Inspiration along the way

It was after his first Shield season that Ricky set his sights on breaking into the Australian team and his guiding light along the way was one of his heroes, David Boon.

'I was lucky in a way because I always had Boonie's path to follow. I had hoped to break into the Australian team when I was twenty and then have a ten to twelve year career ahead of me playing for Australia.

'Boonie played for Tassie at seventeen and I did the same, and so far my career has pretty much followed his. Although he finished with over twenty centuries and I've only got two—I've got a long way to go!

'I always looked up to Boonie and he has been a good role model for me. I was lucky enough to have played my first Shield game with him when I was seventeen and I have no doubt his presence made a difference. It was such a big bonus having someone that I had looked up to for so long as a team-mate.

'But while I look up to Boonie, we have very different styles. I am probably a more aggressive batsman than Boonie was at my age but it is unfair to compare our styles really. He was ranked the best batter in the world at one stage and you don't get that tag unless you've got all the strokes in the book and Boonie definitely had that in his prime.

'I have a long way to go before I am in the same league as far as Test centuries and first-class runs are concerned and nobody will be able to make any real comparison until I have finished playing and by then nobody will give a damn anyway, least of all Boonie or me.'

'I sometimes look back on how I played the game when I first started and how I tackle it now and there is a difference. There was always this hidden pressure on me when I moved closer to breaking into the Shield team and again the season before I made my Test debut.

'I think that the things that Rod Marsh said about me very early on in my career not only made me realise that I had a special gift but it also taught me how to handle the hidden pressures that come with playing at the top level.

'When Marshy went in to bat for me in a big way, some people thought it was putting too much pressure on me, but it was the reverse. It just made me feel good about myself. Rod had played so much cricket and performed so well at the highest level that he was well qualified to make those sort of statements. To have someone like him saying those things about you would make any player feel a bit special.'

Marsh more than once sang Ricky's praises in the press and on television and radio but he was always one for backing the next best thing to a certainty.

Ricky learned from an early age to take things in his stride and getting a swollen head was just not in his kit bag. As he says: 'I never get carried away when something's written in the papers or on television that has the potential to over-pamper my ego. I just reflect back on what the boys from my home club at Mowbray once told me—don't get a big head—and that usually brings me right back down to earth.'

Chapter six

THE FIRST STEPS

THE introduction of an Australian seconds team for the 1995 international one-day series in Australia was met with mixed response from the Australian players.

For the regular members of the Australian team it was considered awkward having to play against their team-mates while it was seen as a fantastic opportunity for the host of fringe players who were waiting in the wings.

Ricky seized the opportunity to play at this level as did players such as Greg Blewett, Justin Langer and Damien Martyn who captained the second-string Aussie line-up.

Ricky's first game, however, was a disaster, being run out for a duck against Zimbabwe. As he says: 'It wasn't the sort of start I was hoping for, but we won the match.

'In the second game I knocked up 31 against England at the MCG and then I got 45 against Australia in Adelaide. I felt pretty good until I hoiked a ball from Warnie over mid-wicket only to be caught right on the boundary.'

The controversy over the value of having two Australian teams in the competition continued to brew, but when the Australia-A team made it into the final with a nail-biting win over England at the SCG the debate hit feverpitch.

'The guys in the Australia-A team were rapt to make the final and we were all fired up to win the best-of-three final.

'We chalked up 270 against England in the last game with Langer and Blewey each making a century. We then had to restrict England from getting within 40 runs of our total which we did and made it through to the finals.

'We lost the first two finals but it was a great experience.'

When the phone call came to advise Ricky he had been selected in an Australian team to contest a four-nation one-day series in New Zealand prior to the West Indies tour, he was shocked. All the hard work and dedication had finally paid off and the door was now open for him to finally achieve what he set out to do when in his last year at Brooks High School.

'It was the day I had been waiting for, but even though I had done well in the Australia-A team in the one-day competition in Australia it really came as a shock.

'We did some celebrating that night and on into the early hours of the morning, and I think I spent the whole of the next day on the telephone.

'It took a while for it to sink in. I knew then that playing Test cricket might not be too far away. Now it was all up to me and how I could handle the step up in class.

'It was a terrific trip because all the players' wives and girlfriends went along—in a way it felt like a holiday. But the opening match was a disaster for me because I only scored one against South Africa at Wellington. I never got much of a chance in the next match against New Zealand going in with only a couple of overs remaining but I finished not out on 10.

'For the game against India I was promoted up the list to first drop and I made 62 which was a fair effort. Then I finished the tour with 7 not out in the final which we won against New Zealand in Auckland.

'It was a terrific fortnight but it was capped when they told me towards the end of the series that I had been selected to go to the West Indies!'

Off to the Caribbean

'When I was selected for the West Indies tour it was like all my birthdays had come at once. I had some reservations about making my Test debut against arguably the best fast bowling attack in the world.

'I was in good form and all I could think about was getting amongst the runs when we hit the Caribbean, although I knew that it wouldn't be easy snaring a Test berth but I was hopeful of playing a few one-day games.

'I was nervous when we arrived at Barbados for our first session in the nets because having good nets was probably going to be the only way I could get a game.

'Things settled down after a few days and rooming with Steve Waugh was a big help. "Tugga" is a quiet sort of bloke who spends most of his spare time working on notes for his tour diaries, but we had a few long conversations and it was interesting to hear who he regarded as the toughest bowlers he had faced, of which one was Curtly Ambrose. We also talked about how he handled the pressure of playing Test cricket.

'I also bunked with Tim May who is, without a doubt,

one of the funniest blokes I have ever met. "Maysie" is always the one to come up with the jokes and is the dead-set life of the party. He is really good at mimicking people and once he gets rolling you just can't stop him.

'On one of our free days we took off to this island and when it was time to head back to the hotel Maysie decided he wanted to kick on and go to a nightclub.

'I was rooming with him and I wasn't too keen to carry on so I went back to my room and he made a night of it.

'He got home at about 5.00 am but was still at the breakfast table with all the guys. Nobody would have guessed that he had tied one on the night before. However, he was a bit concerned about a pair of bathers. He had them on under his pants when he went to the nightclub but he didn't know where they were when he woke up!

'I also roomed with Mark Waugh and Glenn McGrath during the tour, but they were mild compared to what it was like sharing a room with Maysie.'

As the tour progressed Ricky began to realise his chances of padding up for a Test were nearly non-existent, but he was pleased when he was given the nod to bat at number three in the second one-day game at the famed Port-of-Spain oval in Trinidad.

'We were chasing a big total of 300-plus after Brian Lara had belted 139 and when I walked to the crease we were one for bugger-all and Curtly Ambrose was all fired up ready to steam in on a wicket that had heaps of bounce.

'I was expecting a short one but he gave me one at full pitch and I leaned back and struck it in the middle of the bat. It was incredible how quickly the butterflies disappeared.

'I went on to make 43 but we got flogged.'

The next match was at Georgetown on a pitch that was

one of the most placid the team had seen on tour.

'We won the toss and batted and I was moved down the list to number five and as keen as mustard to make the most of the perfect batting strip.

'But I played all over the fourth ball I faced from Carl Hooper and I just managed to get the bottom of the bat on the ball and back went my leg stump. Out for a duck! Hardly the sort of result I was after that day.'

Ricky had another chance to get amongst the runs, against Georgetown in a three-day game against Guyana.

'I had a couple of good nets and I guessed the game against Guyana might be my last chance to get some time in the middle, but I was out for 19 attempting a pull-shot in the first innings and time didn't permit another dig. That was it for me, as far as playing was concerned in the West Indies.'

While his performances from limited opportunities were well below his expectations, the experience he gained from the 10-week tour was priceless.

'The First Test in Barbados was a tremendous experience, even though I was not in the XI. The series was billed as one which would determine the world champions so the boys were really pumped—victory in the First Test would give us a real confidence boost.

'I could feel the tension building in the rooms before the start of play and when the boys hit the field for the first session I took my place in the stand along with Justin Langer and Maysie, hoping for some early breakthroughs.

'Despite sitting in the stand we still felt a part of the action, although I would have killed to have been out there in the middle. I found myself jumping up and shouting along with every appeal for a catch or lbw decision.

'We had them three for 10 and reeling with BJ [Brendan Julien] and Pigeon [Glenn McGrath] right on top in the first session. After we bundled them out for a modest total and replied with a healthy first innings lead, I knew we had the game by the throat.

'We won the Test by 10 wickets and that's when I was introduced to *Under The Southern Cross*, the traditional victory song. Being a part of that for the first time was a very emotional experience. As Boonie jumped up on a table and launched into the first line of the song I could feel the hairs on the back of my neck stand to attention.

'I knew the song was special but I never realised how moving it could be. And to be a part of the team that won back the coveted Sir Frank Worrell Trophy was a real bonus.'

Ricky not only gained valued experience but he also acquired some additional facial hair during the tour, as did most of the players.

'Someone decided that we all should grow some type of facial hair. All our names were thrown into a hat and into another hat went the names of different types of facial growth such as a goatee beard, sideburns, a Hitler moustache, etc.

'The deal was that if anyone attempted to shave their bit of extra growth off without first consulting the "fuzz" committee they would be fined. All fines were placed into a kitty and used at the end of the tour in the bar.

'I picked the goatee and it took so long to grow that for the first few days I was questioned about whether I had shaved. Most of the guys got to a stage where their extra growth looked ridiculous, shaved it off and just put money in the kitty, but I persevered with mine, although it didn't start to look like a beard until near the end of the tour.'

The West Indies tour brought to an end a hectic season and the players relished the ten-day visit to Bermuda to unwind before returning to Australia.

The Young Australians tour of England

No sooner had Ricky arrived back from the West Indies tour than he was preparing for his first tour of England as a member of the Young Australian squad.

The six-week tour was designed to give many of the members of the 13-man squad a taste of English wickets and climate, and for some give them the opportunity to press for future Test selection.

'The line-up was similar to that of the Australia-A team which contested the one-day series in Australia, and all the guys were looking forward to the trip. Especially me because I had heard so much about the English strips and how different they were to the wickets in Australia. The tour was a chance for the young guns of Australian cricket to further stake their claim for a Test berth in the coming Australian season and I was keen to keep my name to the fore. Having not had a lot of time in the middle in the West Indies I saw the England trip as a terrific opportunity to push my case for Test selection.

'The first match was against Somerset at Taunton and I opened the innings. The wicket was slow and had a bit to offer the seamers and spinners, so I took it easy in the first few overs as I tried to come to terms with the variable bounce which was unlike most of the strips we encounter back home.

'I made 54 and felt like I could have made a double ton,

but I mistimed a drive and popped it straight back to the bowler.

'I dropped down the order in the second innings to number four and was unbeaten on 52 when we declared and we bundled them out to win the match.'

Ricky made 4 and 31 in the next match against Glamorgan and followed up with 6 and a well-made 64 in the second dig against Derby at Chesterfield. But by far his best knock was an unbeaten 103 in the first innings against Worcester which lifted his first-class average to 51.85.

'I was reasonably happy with a few of my knocks leading up to the Worcester game but disappointed that I had made a start and not gone on. However, the century made amends for the failures.

'Although I got to 30 in the second innings, I was caught by Australia's Tom Moody who was playing County cricket over there at the time.

'I followed up with 87 against Hampshire at Southampton when I thought I was odds-on to get another ton, but I played across a ball from Udal and was trapped in front.'

Ricky finished the six-week tour with modest totals against Leicester (4 and 1) and 24 in the team's only innings against a Chairman's XI at Edgbaston.

The tour was regarded a big success for the team because they only lost one game. For Ricky it was a great experience, finishing with 560 runs from 12 visits to the crease for an average of almost 47.

'It was a good tour for quick Michael Kasprowicz and batters Matthew Elliott and Justin Langer and no doubt the national selectors would have been impressed with their efforts. Overall it was fun because all the guys had some time to relax and take in some of the sights. I was only disappointed I never got a chance to get to the races. A lot of my friends had told me that the horse and greyhound racing over there is so different to Australia and I was keen to take a look. However, I vowed to do it if, and when, I went back for an Ashes tour.'

Chapter seven

A TEST BERTH AWAITS

WHEN Ricky returned from England there was no time for a break with the first Shield game for Tasmania only eight weeks away. The first game was against NSW at the SCG and Ricky knew the Australian selectors were close to making a decision on whether he would be blooded at Test level that season.

'The first Shield game is always tough but especially so when there is a bit riding on the outcome, on a personal level. I have never been one to play for myself, it has always been the team first, but it does make a difference when you know there is a definite chance of grabbing a Test berth. I made a start in both innings but 20 and 43 was far from what I was looking for and losing the match was an even worse result.'

But back on one of his favourite grounds, Bellerive in Hobart, Ricky staked a serious claim for a Test berth against Sri Lanka in Adelaide in early December.

Against a strong Queensland attack Ricky carved out two unbeaten centuries (118 and 100) to help Tasmania to a resounding win over the Maroons.

'Two centuries was the goal I set before the game because I felt that the only way to really push for a Test berth was to get big runs on the board.'

However, Ricky was not content with those two first-rate knocks; he cut loose against the Sri Lankans in a one-day game for Tasmania on his home turf in Launceston scoring a brilliant 131 not out in front of a very boisterous home crowd. 'There is nothing like making a ton in front of your home crowd and to do it against the Sri Lankans was a bit special.'

The national selectors responded by selecting Ricky for his Test debut against Sri Lanka in Perth a week later.

When he made his way to WA to prepare for his long-awaited Test debut, Ricky was on the verge of becoming only the 11th Tasmanian to play Test cricket for Australia. Ironically the 10th Tasmanian to secure a cap for Australia was none other than Ricky's uncle, Greg Campbell, who made his debut at Lord's in England in 1989. And like Campbell, Ricky was to make his Test debut in a team also boasting Tasmania's favourite cricketing son, David Boon.

The night before, Ricky went out to dinner and then slipped over to the greyhound meeting at Launceston's White City to have a few beers with his mates.

The next day he was on a plane headed for the WACA ground where his future would unfold.

The only disappointing aspect of Ricky's Test debut was that the third day of the First Test against Sri Lanka in

December 1995 did not coincide with his 21st birthday.

Nevertheless, the stage had been set for a dream beginning to a career which looked certain to take the young Tasmanian on a roller-coaster ride to stardom, similar to that enjoyed by David Boon.

'I had been ready to take the step up to Test level for some time but it is very hard to break into an Australian team, especially the Test arena,' Ricky says. 'My form for Tassie in Shield competition was pretty good and having scored 99 in a one-dayer against Sri Lanka at Devonport and my 131 not out against them in a three-day game at the NTCA ground in Launceston a week before the First Test, helped my chances of being selected in the Test team.

'Mind you I was shocked and surprised when I was told I had been selected in the Test team, even though I knew I could handle the step up. I knew that my form was good against the Sri Lankans but you are never really sure of how the selectors are thinking.

'Luckily I knew the WACA strip would give me a real chance to make an impact with the bat in my Test debut.'

The bonus for Ricky was that his place in the Test team was not at the expense of fellow Tasmanian David Boon who had been going through a lean time with the bat.

Australia took to the field first and Ricky found it hard to contain the emotion when he strolled onto the WACA ground at 10.30 am on December 8, 1995.

'I think I had a smile on my dial for the first half-hour we were out there. It was a great feeling soaking up the atmosphere and I kept looking over to where my parents and Nan were sitting, and thought how they must be feeling.

'The excitement wore off after a while and then it was just another game of cricket.

'We dismissed the Sri Lankans for less than 300 which was a good effort on that pitch and then we set about the chase.

'When we lost the first wicket [Taylor] I put my thigh pad and box on, and when Boonie went I put the pads on and assembled the rest of my gear. I made my usual trip to the toilet before I padded up but that day I probably wore a path to the loo!

'The boys were batting well and Slats looked real good. Junior and he were locked into a solid partnership.

'As the day wore on I became more nervous, especially the last hour before the close of play. I wasn't sure whether I would have to go out there and bat, and that was playing on my mind, but when I saw the night watchman padded up it calmed me a bit.

'I went out to dinner that night with Mum and Dad and I felt fairly relaxed, but when I got back to my room and slipped into bed it seemed like ages before I dropped off to sleep. The next morning I went through the normal drill, but I wasn't as nervous as the previous day.

'When I got to the crease we were in good shape at four for 350-odd. The first ball I faced from off-spinner Muttiah Muralitharan was a ripper that caught the outside edge and went devilishly close to the first slipper's grasp but then it went for four. It's the same feeling at Test level as it is in junior competition when you nick the first ball and it goes to the boundary—you feel lucky straightaway.'

Ricky nervously made his way to 13 but a pull-shot which went scurrying to the mid-wicket boundary seemed to lift his confidence. 'It took me a few overs to get settled but once I middled that pull-shot it was like slipping into another gear. I felt very comfortable using my feet to the spinners and by the time I reached 30 I was right in the zone. Once a batsman is in the zone there seems to be so much more time to get into position to play shots—finding the middle of the bat is a formality.

'Reaching 50 was a tremendous feeling and all I could think of doing when I reached the other end was to turn towards my family who had travelled to Perth for the match and raise my bat to them, and to Mum in particular.

'There had been so much expected of me and even though I ignored most of what was written in the newspapers, it was difficult to avoid all of it and that added to the pressure. However, everything was going along smoothly and Stuart Law and I had put on quite a respectable partnership and it wasn't until I got to 80 that I felt confident about reaching a century.'

But for Ricky, it wasn't to be. 'I was on 96 and Chaminda Vaas got one to cut back and lift sharply on me and the ball hit me very high up on the leg, near the groin region. All I could hear was this almighty loud appeal ringing in my ears.

'Every time a batsman gets rapped on the pads he panics and I had that feeling for a split second, but I felt sure the ball had hit me too high up and was definitely going over the stumps.

'But when I looked up and saw the umpire's finger I was shocked, then I felt more disappointed because I had worked so bloody hard to be within a boundary of reaching the ton. But soon after in the rooms I realised that I had done a good job for the team. And had someone told me before the game that I could have 96 on my Test debut I would have taken it.

'I watched the replay a couple of times in the dressing room and it was obvious that the ball would have gone well over the stumps but no matter what we all might have thought, the scorebook has the final say in this game.'

Some bookmakers had set the odds as high as 33–1 on Ponting scoring a century on debut. A few of his family and close friends had parted with some hard-earned cash at the juicy odds.

As Ricky jokes: 'If I had known those odds were on offer I would have had a few dollars on myself.'

The crowd at the WACA turned quite hostile towards umpire Hayat, especially after replays of Ricky's dismissal had been shown on monitors a few times in the various grandstands around the ground.

'A lot was said about the dismissal but the umpire has a job to do and as far as he was concerned I was out and that's the end of it.

'I reckon there will be a few lbw decisions go my way in the future and I'll probably be on the receiving end of more dubious ones, but that's just the way it goes in this game.

'I went out to dinner that night with my parents and Nan, and by the time I sat down to eat, the disappointment of having failed by only four runs had gone and I was comfortable with the fact that I had done very well on debut.'

Ricky went on to take three catches in Sri Lanka's second innings with Australia cruising to a comfortable victory without the young Tasmanian having to take guard in the second innings.

'Despite missing my century it was a very satisfying Test debut for me and all I could think about was going to Melbourne for the Second Test at the MCG.

'Winning by an innings was a tremendous effort and there were plenty of great individual performances in the match. Warnie snared his 200th Test wicket in only his 42nd Test and McGrath signalled his arrival as a genuine Test class quick with four first-innings wickets and three in the second. Slats answered his critics with a fantastic double ton (219) in the first innings. Stuart Law did a great job to be unbeaten on 54 and we shared an unbeaten sixth-wicket stand of 121.

'But the Sri Lankans didn't give up without a fight in their second innings and Tillakaratne's 119 was a gutsy knock.

'Someone asked me after the match whether I had achieved my goal and I couldn't help but reflect back on my days at the AIS Academy. We had sessions on goal setting and it was fairly heavy stuff, and I can remember after a few sessions I told Rod Marsh that according to what we had just gone through in the sessions I had probably never ever set goals in my life.

'Rod explained to me that I had been setting goals all of my life except I was going about it differently to most people. After all I had set my sights on playing for Australia by the time I was twenty-three and that would have given me a five-year apprenticeship in Shield competition.

'But I was one of the lucky ones who got the breaks when they counted and made the most of the opportunities when they came along.'

In a game in which run rates rule supreme, a cricketer's daring is obligatory and field placings are often far-fetched,

FIRST TEST—AUSTRALIA v SRI LANKA
WACA Ground, Perth. December 8, 9, 10, 11, 1995
Toss: Sri Lanka. Result: Australia won by an innings & 36 runs

Stumps Scores: Day 1: S.L (1) 251 all out; Day 2: Aus (1) 2/358 (Slater 189, Waugh 36); Day 3: S.L (2) 0/13 (Mahanama 2, Hathurusinghe 7).

SRI LANKA

FIRST INNINGS	RUNS	SECOND INNINGS	RUNS
RS Mahanama c Warne b McDermott	15	b McGrath	48
UC Hathurusinghe c Law b McGrath	14	c Healy b McGrath	11
AP Gurinsinha b McGrath	46	c Healy b McDermott	7
PA De Silva c & b Warne	10	c Ponting b Warne	20
A Ranatunga* c Healy b McGrath	32	b McGrath	46
HP Tillekeratne lbw McDermott	6	c Ponting b Warne	119
RS Kaluwitharana† c Taylor b Warne	50	c Ponting b Julian	40
HDPK Dharmasena b McDermott	30	lbw McDermott	18
WPUJC Vaas c Healy b Warne	4	c Healy b Warne	4
GP Wickramasinghe c Julian b McGrath	28	c Warne b McDermott	0
M Muralitharan not out	0	not out	3
Sundries (B 4, LB 9, NB 3)	16	(LB 4, NB 10)	14
TOTAL	251		330

F/W 25 38 54 129 132 172 193 205 251 251

35 56 87 105 193 258 310 318 319 330

Bowler	Ovrs	Mdns	Runs	Wkts	NB	W
FIRST INNINGS						
McDermott	18.4	5	44	3		
McGrath	24	3	81	4	1	—
Julian	17	8	32	0		
Warne	27	7	75	3	2	—
Waugh	3	1	6	0		
SECOND INNINGS						
McGrath	24	7	86	3		
McDermott	20	3	73	3	10	—
Warne	29.4	6	96	3		
Julian	13	4	40	1		
Waugh	4	0	22	0		
Law	3	1	9	0		

AUSTRALIA

FIRST INNINGS	RUNS
MJ Slater c & b Muralitharan	219
MA Taylor* lbw De Silva	96
DC Boon c Hathurusinghe b Muralitharan	13
ME Waugh c Kaluwitharana b Vaas	111
RT Ponting lbw VAAS	96
SG Law not out	54
IA Healy†	
BP Julian	
SK Warne	
CJ McDermott	
GD McGrath	
Sundries (B 4, LB 6, NB 18)	28
TOTAL	5 dec 617

F/W 228 266 422 496 617

Bowler	Ovrs	Mdns	Runs	Wkts	NB	W
FIRST INNINGS						
Wickramasinghe	31	3	123	0	7	—
Vaas	31	5	103	2	3	—
Muralitharan	54	3	224	2	4	—
Hathurusinghe	9	3	31	0		
Dharmasena	31	5	84	0		
De Silva	18	1	42	1	4	—

Umpires: Khizer Hayat & PD Parker (TV Umpire—BT Rennie)
Referee: GT Dowling
12th Men: MS Kasprowicz (Australia) & ST Jayasuriya (Sri Lanka)
Man of Match: MJ Slater (Australia)

it should come as no surprise that the flashier one-day game at international level has pushed Test cricket to the outer. One-day cricket has taken over the mantle as the most popular form of cricket and Ricky's cavalier style of batting and panther-like athleticism in the field has made him one of the stars.

With the First Test over and hangovers from victory celebrations only a blur in the players' minds, Australia turned its attention to winning the World Series against Sri Lanka and the West Indies.

Ricky had only a handful of international limited-over games to his credit, including a series on home soil for Australia-A, four outings in the Centenary series in New Zealand and two on the West Indies tour. But form was on his side and he now had the opportunity to further stake his claim as a genuine international cricketer.

'I went into the first limited-over game against the West Indies full of confidence but I started poorly with a paltry 11 against the West Indies in Adelaide, followed up with six against them in Melbourne.

'My performances against the West Indies weren't crash hot but after talking with a few of my team-mates I realised

AUSTRALIA v WEST INDIES
Adelaide Oval, Adelaide. December 17, 1995
Toss: West Indies. Result: Australia won by 121 runs

AUSTRALIA	Runs	Min	Bls	4s	6s
MA Taylor* b Harper	47	103	91	4	—
MJ Slater b Bishop	32	57	40	4	1
ME Waugh c Hooper b Harper	53	98	65	3	—
RT Ponting st Browne b Harper	11	28	21	—	—
SG Law c Hooper b Harper	13	17	19	—	—
MG Bevan not out	32	38	27	4	—
S Lee st Browne b Hooper	39	29	27	3	—
IA Healy† not out	0	2	1	—	—
SK Warne					
CJ McDermott					
GD McGrath					
Sundries (B 1, LB 7, W 7)	15				
TOTAL (Overs: 47.0—Mins: 189)	6 for 242				

F/W 60 108 142 166 169 232

Bowler	Ovrs	Mdns	Runs	Wkts	NB	W
Ambrose	9	—	43	—	—	4
Walsh	10	1	46	—	—	—
Bishop	8	—	33	1	—	1
Simmons	2	—	17	—	—	—
Hooper	8	—	49	1	—	1
Harper	10	—	46	4	—	1

WEST INDIES	Runs	Min	Bls	4s	6s
PV Simmons c Waugh b McGrath	7	23	20	1	—
SL Campbell run out (McDermott)	4	11	10	1	—
RB Richardson* c Healy b McDermott	4	15	5	—	—
CL Hooper lbw McDermott	0	14	10	—	—
S Chanderpaul c Taylor b Waugh	39	111	83	—	—
JC Adams c Law b Lee	20	48	46	1	—
RA Harper not out	31	84	82	1	—
CO Browne† not out	11	32	30	—	—
CEL Ambrose					
IR Bishop					
CA Walsh					
Sundries (LB 2, W 3)	5				
TOTAL (Overs: 47.0—Mins: 172)	6 for 121				

F/W 8 16 16 17 54 97

Bowler	Ovrs	Mdns	Runs	Wkts	NB	W
McDermott	7	2	8	2	—	1
McGrath	5	1	13	1	—	1
Law	7	1	23	—	—	—
Lee	7	—	20	1	—	—
Waugh	10	—	26	1	—	—
Warne	7	1	22	—	—	1
Bevan	3	—	7	—	—	—
Slater	1	1	0	—	—	—

Umpires: AJ McQuillan & TA Prue (TV Umpire—SJ Davis)
Referee: GT Dowling
12th Men: MS Kasprowicz (Australia) & SC Williams (West Indies)
Man of Match: ME Waugh

that I was probably putting a bit too much pressure on myself. Maybe it was a case of trying to make up for not getting a hundred in my first test.

'But things picked up in the next game against Sri Lanka. I scored 56 batting at my set position at number four. Then because I had done well against Sri Lanka all season, I was very determined to get at least one good score against the Windies before the finals.'

Ricky's performances with the bat in the Second Test of the series against Sri Lanka at the MCG confirmed he was worthy of the transition from Shield to Test level.

His 71 from 167 balls in the first innings was crafted in workmanlike fashion and peppered with classic drives, powerful pull and hook shots, and possibly the best cover drive of the series.

'There was always the chance that I would fail in the Second Test and I was very determined to ensure my effort in the First Test wasn't overshadowed by a failure in Melbourne.'

It was a sensational Test match because Sri Lankan off-spinner Murriah Muralitharan was no-balled by umpire Darrell Hair for throwing. Hair called him seven times in three overs before he was taken out of the attack.

Muralitharan became only the third Test bowler to be called for throwing in Australia after Ernie Jones (1897–98) and left-arm quick Ian Meckiff (1963–64).

'The other umpire in the match, Steve Dunne, was okay with Muralitharan's action but Hair said he would start no-balling the bowler from square-leg if he bowled after the tea break and he never bowled another ball in the match.

'I shared a good 115-run partnership with Steve Waugh

SECOND TEST—AUSTRALIA v SRI LANKA
MCG, Melbourne. December 26, 27, 28, 29, 30, 1995
Toss: Sri Lanka. Result: Australia won by 10 wickets

Stumps Scores: Day 1: Aus (1) 3/234 (Boon 93, SR Waugh 2); Day 2: S.L (1) 1/29 (Hathurusinghe 16, Gurinsinha 10); Day 3: S.L (2) 1/33 (Hathurusinghe 20, Gurinsinha 0); Day 4: S.L (2) 6/284 (Ranatunga 6, Vaas 5).

AUSTRALIA

FIRST INNINGS	RUNS		SECOND INNINGS	RUNS
MJ Slater c Wickramasinghe b Vaas	62	(2)	not out	13
MA Taylor* b Wickramasinghe	7	(1)	not out	25
DC Boon c Muralitharan b Wickramasinghe	110			
ME Waugh b Muralitharan	61			
SR Waugh not out	131			
RT Ponting c Gurinsinha b Silva	71			
IA Healy† c Muralitharan b De Silva	41			
PR Reiffel not out	4			
SK Warne				
CJ McDermott				
GD McGrath				
Sundries (LB 8, W 2, NB 3)	13		(LB 1, NB 2)	3
TOTAL	6 dec 500			0 for 41

F/W 14 116 219 280 395 488

Bowler	Ovrs	Mdns	Runs	Wkts	NB	W
FIRST INNINGS						
Wickramasinghe	30.2	9	77	2	1	2
Vaas	40.4	11	93	1	1	—
Hathurusinghe	9	0	23	0		
Gurinsinha	2	0	8	0		
Muralitharan	38	7	124	1	1	—
Silva	35	5	120	1		
De Silva	10	0	47	1		
SECOND INNINGS						
Vaas	3	0	25	0	2	
Gurinsinha	3	1	6	0		
De Silva	1	0	4	0		
Tillekeratne	0.4	0	5	0		

SRI LANKA

FIRST INNINGS	RUNS		SECOND INNINGS	RUNS
RS Mahanama c Taylor b McGrath	3		c Warne b Reiffel	3
UC Hathurusinghe lbw McGrath	23		lbw Warne	39
AP Gurinsinha c Healy b Ponting	27		lbw Reiffel	143
PA De Silva c Reiffel b McGrath	18		c Healy b McDermott	28
A Ranatunga* c Warne b McDermott	51	(7)	not out	11
HP Tillekeratne c Taylor b Warne	14		c Ponting b ME Waugh	38
RS Kaluwitharana c Boon b McDermott†	50	(5)	st Healy b Warne	2
WPUJC Vaas c Healy b Reiffel	0		c Boon b McGrath	6
GP Wickramasinghe c Healy b McGrath	10		st Healy b Warne	17
M. Muralitharan c Slater b McGrath	11		c Taylor b Warne	0
KJ Silva not out	6		b McGrath	0
Sundries (B 6, LB 7, NB 7)	20		(B 7, LB 5, W 8)	20
TOTAL	233			307

F/W 3 64 68 128 140 182 183 213 221 233

11 97 168 172 255 273 285 306 306 307

Bowler	Ovrs	Mdns	Runs	Wkts	NB	W
FIRST INNINGS						
McDermott	23	8	63	2	5	—
McGrath	23.4	9	40	5		
Reiffel	20	5	60	1	2	—
Ponting	4	2	8	1		
Warne	18	5	49	1		
SECOND INNINGS						
McGrath	33.5	6	92	2		
McDermott	17	1	54	1	—	4
Reiffel	20	7	59	2	—	4
Warne	37	10	71	4		
ME Waugh	9	1	19	1		

Umpires: RS Dunne & DB Hair (TV Umpire—WP Sheahan)
Referee: GT Dowling
12th Men: MS Kasprowicz (Australia) & ST Jayasuriya (Sri Lanka)
Man of Match: GD McGrath (Australia)

who was undefeated on 131 when Tubby declared at 6–500.

'We knocked them over for 233 on the third day and the star was definitely McGrath who got his first five-haul ending up with 5 for 40 and that was probably the best I had ever seen him bowl.

'They had to follow on and we grabbed a wicket before the close of play and we felt confident we could knock them over with a day to spare, but Gurusinha had other ideas and he showed a lot of fight scoring 143, and they ended the fourth day at 6 for 284 and an overall lead of 17 with four wickets in hand.

'In the first session the next day we cleaned them up within twenty minutes and Slats and Tubby had no trouble in scoring the required runs to give us a convincing ten-wicket victory.

'I felt comfortable with how I had settled into Test cricket but I knew that there was a long road ahead before I could class myself a genuine Test player. After all I failed in both innings of the Third Test in Adelaide and that was very disheartening. But in this game you have to quickly come to terms with failure so that you can focus on the next innings.

'But we won the match and the series three-nil, and Steve Waugh's performance with the bat and ball easily earned him the player of the series award.'

Ricky finally found his touch against the West Indies with a solid 61 at the 'Gabba which preceded his best knock of the series in Melbourne against Sri Lanka in which he notched his maiden century for Australia. There's nothing like scoring a century and to notch my first in one-day internationals at the MCG was a bonus.

'I am usually oblivious to crowd noise because the concentration level is so high that you have to block out the crowd otherwise it becomes too much of a distraction, but it was a real buzz when the huge crowd erupted when I brought up my ton.

'I had been very disappointed in not getting my 100 on debut and again in the Second Test when it was there for the taking.

'We were in a bit of strife early losing three wickets cheaply and then Bevo [Michael Bevan] and I put on over 200 for the fourth wicket, and I rate it as one of the best partnerships I've been involved in.

'I had found the middle early and cracked a few fours, but when we lost those quick wickets we had to make sure we steadied the ship. Bevo and I just worked the ball around pretty much for 20-odd overs and it was only towards the end that I opened up again.

AUSTRALIA v WEST INDIES
Brisbane Cricket Ground, Brisbane. January 7, 1996
Toss: Australia. Result: West Indies won by 14 runs

WEST INDIES	Runs	Min	Bls	4s	6s
SC Williams c Healy b McGrath	0	2	3	—	—
SL Campbell b McGrath	5	31	19	—	—
PV Simmons c Lee b Waugh	42	92	64	2	1
RB Richardson* c Bevan b Law	81	128	111	6	2
CL Hooper c Slater b Reiffel	18	21	19	3	—
RA Harper b Waugh	10	31	22	—	—
CO Browne† run out (Ponting/Law)	1	3	4	—	—
OD Gibson b Lee	52	48	40	4	2
IR Bishop run out (Ponting/Lee)	5	31	16	—	—
CEL Ambrose not out	3	14	8	—	—
CA Walsh b McGrath	0	4	4	—	—
Sundries (LB 3, W 6, NB 5)	14				
TOTAL (Overs: 49.3—Mins: 207)	231				

F/W 2 27 103 133 167 169 173 220 230 231

Bowler	Ovrs	Mdns	Runs	Wkts	NB	W
McGrath	9.3	1	47	3	1	2
Reiffel	7	1	50	1	1	1
McDermott	8	—	43	—	3	—
Waugh	10	—	30	2	—	—
Bevan	3	—	16	—	—	1
Lee	8	1	30	1	—	2
Law	4	1	12	1	—	—

AUSTRALIA	Runs	Min	Bls	4s	6s
MA Taylor* c Browne b Bishop	14	37	20	2	—
MJ Slater c Campbell b Ambrose	0	3	4	—	—
ME Waugh c Browne b Walsh	5	10	11	—	—
RT Ponting c Harper b Bishop	61	116	86	4	1
SG Law c & b Simmons	62	130	99	3	—
MG Bevan run out (RIC Holder)	17	40	32	—	—
S Lee c Simmons b Walsh	6	12	11	1	—
IA Healy† c Walsh b Gibson	15	35	24	1	—
PR Reiffel run out (Richardson)	14	22	12	1	—
CJ McDermott b Gibson	1	5	2	—	—
GD McGrath not out	0	1	0	—	—
Sundries (LB 6, W 7, NB 9)	22				
TOTAL (Overs: 47.4—Mins: 210)	217				

F/W 1 10 27 142 179 180 187 216 217 217

Bowler	Ovrs	Mdns	Runs	Wkts	NB	W
Ambrose	9	2	20	1	1	—
Walsh	9	—	56	2	2	—
Bishop	10	—	49	2	1	6
Gibson	5.4	—	38	2	5	1
Harper	4	1	9	—	—	—
Simmons	10	—	39	1	—	—

Umpires: DB Hair & PD Parker (TV Umpire—AJ McQuillan)
Referee: GT Dowling
12th Men: SK Warne (Australia) & JC Adams (West Indies)
Man of Match: OD Gibson

'I felt sick in the stomach when I was run out but at that stage of the innings we had to go for it and that's part of the beauty of one-day cricket. The most disappointing aspect was losing the game.'

Ricky finished the World Series with 341 runs for an average of 34.10 and a strike rate of almost 74.

Chapter eight

THE WORLD CUP CONTROVERSY

RICKY'S selection in the 14-man squad for the World Cup in Sri Lanka and India in February 1996, was a formality. His performance in the Tests and limited-over internationals made him more than worthy of another trip abroad.

But controversy struck the team before the ink had even dried on the overseas travel documents.

About three weeks before the series was to start, a Tamil Tiger suicide bomber had driven a truckload of explosives into the nine-storey Central Bank in the heart of the city centre in Colombo. The bombing killed 80 people and injured over 1000.

Australia and the West Indies were to play Sri Lanka in Colombo in the opening matches of the tournament and news of the bombing immediately put the World Cup in jeopardy.

Ricky was concerned over the bombing but he did not believe that the tournament should be cancelled or that Australia should not participate. As he says: 'The bombing was a tragedy and there is no doubt the atmosphere in Colombo at the time was horrendous but a lot of the players were still keen to proceed with the original schedule.

'However, many Australian players who were to make the trip, including Shane Warne, Mark Waugh and Ian Healy, had been the target of personal death threats from people claiming to be associated with the Tamil separatist group. These stemmed from previous games between Australia and Sri Lanka, but mainly the Arjuna Ranatunga affair.

'All the players met a few times with members of the Australian Cricket Board to try and sort out the mess, but every time we seemed to have the right solution there would be another twist or turn in Colombo which would reverse the decision.'

Almost two weeks after the tragic bombing in Colombo, Sri Lankan police discovered a truck, similar to the one used in the suicide bombing, parked outside a Buddhist temple and loaded with 250kg of explosives.

'When we learned that another truckload of explosives had been found and that there was plenty of uncertainty about how tight the security would be for the players over there, we called more urgent meetings with the ACB,' Ricky says. 'The ACB tried to convince the tournament organisers to transfer the Colombo games to India but they wouldn't budge. In the end they made the decision that Australia would forfeit the first game against Sri Lanka and the West Indies followed suit.'

Sri Lanka was awarded four points for the two forfeited games on their home turf but the furore continued with threats by the tournament organisers of further repercussions.

A solidarity match was arranged by the organisers between Sri Lanka and a combined India-Pakistan line-up. This would serve as some consolation for the cricket-crazed Sri Lankans who would have crammed into the Colombo stadium like sardines to see their country play against Australia and the West Indies. Some newspaper reports suggested the solidarity match, in effect, had branded the Australians and West Indians nothing more than a bunch of wimps.

'Being called a pack of wimps didn't bother any of us and I'm sure it was the same for the West Indian players. I was comfortable with the final decision that was made and after all, our safety was the prime concern. Had we played that match in Colombo and something terrible happened, the ACB would have copped it in the neck.

'The fact was there was a chance that members of our team may have been hurt or killed, so it wasn't worth the risk.'

Australian fast bowler Craig McDermott and his family were put through a harrowing ordeal prior to the team leaving Australia for the World Cup.

A man had telephoned Queensland cricket officials and told them that a bomb had been planted at McDermott's family home on the Gold Coast because of his association with the Australian cricket team and the forthcoming visit to Sri Lanka.

'When people start sending death threats and worrying the hell out of your family that's going too far. Had I been in the same situation as Craig, I too would have had grave fears about playing in Colombo.'

Tournament secretary Jagmohan Dalmiya was reported as saying that should a similar incident have taken place in London it would not have stopped the India team touring England later that year. Dalmiya was also quoted as saying

India would never bow to the threat of terrorism which tears at the fabric of mankind.

'It was okay for the tournament organisers to make all those statements, but the Tamil movement had shown no remorse when it accepted responsibility for the bombing,' Ricky says. 'The bomb blast that killed all those people was within a block of the hotel in which our team was scheduled to stay. There were innocent bystanders killed or hurt in the blast and we could just as easily have been in that position ourselves had we gone.'

The Australia team departed for India under a cloud and there were grave doubts whether the players would stand up to the pressure of playing in a region of the world where there was growing animosity towards them.

'On arrival in Calcutta it was clear that security was the tournament organisers' number one priority. There were thousands of people at the airport to greet us but the guards and police kept them well away. It was a weird experience and made us feel like pop stars.

'The buses that took us to the hotel were flanked by police cars and when we checked into the hotel there were guards on patrol in the corridors outside every room. We all felt quite safe but at the same time restricted. Although we all agreed it was better to be safe than sorry.

'The next day we attended the opening ceremony and as far as our part was concerned it went off without a hitch, but the ceremony itself didn't quite go to plan.

'There were a lot of cock-ups like the announcer introducing the wrong teams when they walked onto the oval and the girls who led us into our positions on the field were dressed in jeans and T-shirts because the saris they had had specially made for the ceremony hadn't arrived.

But once all that was over we were back to the hotel and the next day we took off for Bombay where we were to prepare for our first game of the tournament against Kenya.'

A stomach bug, not uncommon on the subcontinent, sidelined Ricky for a day but he recovered and set about

AUSTRALIA v KENYA
Visakhapatnam. February 23 1996
(Group A, match 6)
Toss: Kenya. Result: Australia won by 97 runs

AUSTRALIA		KENYA	
MA Taylor* c Modi b Suji	6	K Otieno† b McGrath	85
ME Waugh c Suji b Ali	130	D Chudasama c Healy b McDermott	5
RT Ponting c Otieno b Ali	6	S Tikolo c Ponting b Reiffel	6
SR Waugh c & b Suji	82	M Odumbe* c Reiffel b Bevan	50
SG Law run out	35	H Modi b Bevan	10
MC Bevan b Ali	12	E Odumbe c Bevan b Reiffel	14
IA Healy† c E Odumbe b Karim	17	D Tikolo not out	11
PR Reiffel not out	3	T Odoyo st Healy b Warne	10
SK Warne not out	0	M Suji not out	1
CJ McDermott		AV Karim	
GD McGrath		R Ali	
Sundries (LB 1, W 10, NB 2)	13	Sundries (LB 7, W 6, NB 2)	15
TOTAL (Overs: 50.0—Mins: 214)	7 for 304	TOTAL (Overs: 50.0—Mins: 215)	7 for 207

F/W 10 26 233 237 261 301 301

F/W 12 30 132 167 188 195 206

Bowler	Ovrs	Mdns	Runs	Wkts	NB	W
KENYA						
Suji	10	1	55	2	—	—
Ali	10	0	45	3	—	—
Odoyo	8	0	58	0	—	—
E Odumbe	4	0	21	0	—	—
Karim	10	1	54	1	—	—
M Odumbe	4	0	35	0	—	—
D Tikolo	3	0	21	0	—	—
S Tikolo	1	0	14	0	—	—

Bowler	Ovrs	Mdns	Runs	Wkts	NB	W
AUSTRALIA						
McDermott	3	0	12	1	—	—
Reiffel	7	1	18	2	—	—
McGrath	10	0	44	1	—	—
SR Waugh	7	0	43	0	—	—
Warne	10	1	25	1	—	—
Bevan	8	0	35	2	—	—
ME Waugh	5	0	23	0	—	—

Punter—First Tests of a Champion

finding some form in the nets and in a practice game prior to the match against Kenya.

'Most of the guys got a bug of some description, it is just part of the deal over there, but when I felt better I had a good knock in a practice game.

'We split the team in half and made up the balance in each side from local cricketers and while it was a lot of fun it served as a real good hit-out because it seemed as if we

INDIA v AUSTRALIA
Bombay, India. February 27 1996
(Group A, match 9)
Toss: Australia. Result: Australia won by 16 runs

AUSTRALIA
ME Waugh run out	126
MA Taylor* c Srinath b Raju	59
RT Ponting c Manjrekar b Raju	12
SR Waugh run out	7
SG Law c & b Kumble	21
MG Bevan run out	6
S Lee run out	9
IA Healy† c Kumble b Prasad	6
SK Warne c Azharuddin b Prasad	0
DW Fleming run out	0
GD McGrath not out	0
Sundries (LB 8, NB 2, W 2)	12
TOTAL (Overs: 50.0)	258

F/W 103 140 157 232 237 244 258 258 258 258

INDIA
AD Jadeja lbw Fleming	1
SR Tendulkar st Healy b ME Waugh	90
VG Kambli b Fleming	0
M Azharuddin* b Fleming	10
SV Manjrekar c Healy b SR Waugh	62
M Prabhakar run out	3
NR Mongia† c Taylor b Warne	27
AR Kumble b Fleming	17
J Srinath c Lee b Fleming	7
V Prasad c Bevan b SR Waugh	0
SLV Raju not out	3
Sundries (B 5, LB 8, NB 1, W 8)	21
TOTAL (Overs: 48.0) 7 for	242

F/W 7 7 70 143 147 201 205 224 231 242

Bowler	Ovrs	Mdns	Runs	Wkts	NB	W
INDIA						
Prabhakar	10	0	55	0	—	—
Srinath	10	1	51	0	—	—
Prasad	10	0	49	2	—	—
Kumble	10	1	47	1	—	—
Raju	10	0	48	2	—	—

Bowler	Ovrs	Mdns	Runs	Wkts	NB	W
AUSTRALIA						
McGrath	8	3	48	0	—	—
Fleming	9	0	36	5	—	—
Warne	10	1	28	1	—	—
Lee	3	0	23	0	—	—
ME Waugh	10	0	44	1	—	—
Bevan	5	0	28	0	—	—
SR Waugh	3	0	22	2	—	—

had been waiting forever to play a game of cricket. I made 72 off about 80 balls although Paul Reiffel got me in the end trying to loft him over long-on.

'But for all the good it did me, I failed miserably in the opening game against Kenya making a paltry six while everyone else scored big time. We won the match but I was a bit cut up at the end of the day.

'The next game against India at Mumbai wasn't much better because I only made 12 but I got out to an absolute blinder of a catch by Manjrekar at backward point.

'I didn't quite time a square drive but it took off like a rocket, and Manjrekar took a dive and stuck his hand out real low and pulled off a pearler, much to my disgust!'

The team had a three day break before taking on Zimbabwe at Nagpur and Ricky again got a bout of gastro.

'They say you become immune to the stomach viruses after a while but I don't think that's possible,' he says.

AUSTRALIA v ZIMBABWE
Nagpur, India. March 1 1996
(Group A, match 11)
Toss: Zimbabwe. Result: Australia won by 8 wickets

ZIMBABWE		AUSTRALIA	
AC Waller run out	67	MA Taylor* c B Strang b PA Strang	34
GW Flower† b McGrath	4	ME Waugh not out	76
GJ Whittall c & b SR Waugh	6	RT Ponting c & b PA Strang	33
ADR Campbell c ME Waugh b SR Waugh	5	SR Waugh not out	5
A Flower* st Healy b Warne	7	SG Law	
CN Evans c Healy b Warne	18	MG Bevan	
HH Streak c SR Waugh b Fleming	13	S Lee	
PA Strang not out	16	IA Healy†	
B Strang b Fleming	0	SK Warne	
SG Peall c Healy b Warne	0	DW Fleming	
C Lock b Warne	5	GD McGrath	
Sundries (LB 8, W 3, NB 2)	13	Sundries (B 6, LB 2, W 1, NB 1)	10
TOTAL (Overs: 45.3)	154	TOTAL (Overs: 36.0)	2 for 158
F/W 21 41 55 68 105 126 140 140 145 154		F/W 92 150	

81

Bowler	Ovrs	Mdns	Runs	Wkts	NB	W
AUSTRALIA						
McGrath	8	2	12	1	—	—
Fleming	9	1	30	2	—	—
Lee	4	2	8	0	—	—
SR Waugh	7	2	22	2	—	—
Warne	9.3	1	34	4	—	—
ME Waugh	5	0	30	0	—	—
Law	3	0	10	0	—	—

Bowler	Ovrs	Mdns	Runs	Wkts	NB	W
ZIMBABWE						
Streak	10	3	29	0	—	—
Lock	4	0	25	0	—	—
B Strang	3	0	20	0	—	—
Whittall	2	0	11	0	—	—
PA Strang	10	2	33	2	—	—
Peall	4	0	20	0	—	—
GW Flower	3	0	12	0	—	—

However, Ricky made a more creditable 33 against Zimbabwe and helped keep Australia's unbeaten record at the tournament intact.

'My knock against Zimbabwe wasn't too bad and I was out to a decent ball that nipped back a bit and I got a leading edge and popped it straight back to the bowler Paul Strang.'

The Zimbabwe innings primed Ricky for a personal best against the West Indies.

'We were keyed up about the West Indies game but except for my 61 in Brisbane the previous time we met my record against them wasn't flash.

'It was a good batting strip but Tubby went early and Courtney Walsh and Curtly Ambrose were right on a length and kept us to 20-odd from the first 10 overs. Slowly but surely we picked up the run rate and when Steve Waugh came in we pushed things along and shared a good partnership.

'I moved into the 90s and the old heart started to pound and then a loose delivery later I had my first century against the Windies.

'It was great to finally crack a ton against them and break the hoodoo. I was run out for 102 and you would think 250 would be a winable score but Richie Richardson spoiled the party with a well-made hundred which won them the game.

'I had a chance to send him back to the pavilion when he was in the 80s. He skied one to deep mid-wicket which I caught but I was too close to the boundary rope and went crashing over the rope and into the sponsor signs, and it was a six instead of out.'

Australia won its quarter-final against New Zealand at Chennai, with Ricky scoring 31, which paved the way for the Australians to meet the West Indies in the semi-final at Chandigarh.

AUSTRALIA v WEST INDIES
Jaipur, India. March 4 1996
(Group A, match 13)
Toss: Australia. Result: West Indies won by 4 wickets

AUSTRALIA		WEST INDIES	
ME Waugh st Browne b Harper	30	ST Campbell† c Healy b Fleming	1
MA Taylor* c Browne b Walsh	9	CO Browne* run out	10
RT Ponting run out	102	BC Lara c McGrath b ME Waugh	60
SR Waugh b Walsh	57	RB Richardson* not out	93
MG Bevan run out	2	S Chanderpaul b ME Waugh	10
SG Law not out	12	RA Harper lbw Reiffel	22
IA Healy† run out	3	KLT Arthurton lbw ME Waugh	0
PR Reiffel not out	4	JC Adams not out	17
SK Warne		IR Bishop	
DW Fleming		CEL Ambrose	
GD McGrath		CA Walsh	
Sundries (LB 3, W 6, NB 1)	10	Sundries (LB 12, W 5, NB 2)	19
TOTAL (Overs: 50)	6 for 229	TOTAL (Overs: 48.5)	6 for 232
F/W 22 84 194 200 216 224		F/W 1 26 113 146 194 196	

Bowler	Ovrs	Mdns	Runs	Wkts	NB	W
WEST INDIES						
Ambrose	10	4	25	0	—	—
Walsh	9	2	35	2	—	—
Bishop	9	0	52	0	—	—
Harper	10	0	46	1	—	—
Arthurton	9	0	53	0	—	—
Adams	3	0	15	0	—	—

Bowler	Ovrs	Mdns	Runs	Wkts	NB	W
AUSTRALIA						
Reiffel	10	2	45	1	—	—
Fleming	7.5	1	44	1	—	—
McGrath	9	0	46	0	—	—
Warne	10	1	30	0	—	—
ME Waugh	10	1	38	3	—	—
Bevan	2	0	17	0	—	—

Australia batted first but were in trouble early with Mark Waugh and Ricky failing to score and Taylor (1) and Steve Waugh (3) also back in the pavilion.

It was left to Stuart Law and Michael Bevan, who came together with the score at 4 for 15, to steer Australia out of the mire.

As Ricky remembers: 'Law went on to make 72 and Bevo 69 and Healy chimed in for a well-made 31 to give us a slim chance of victory. The Windies had 208 to get to give them a berth in the final.

'They got off to a fair start with Courtney Browne and Chanderpaul opening but we made a breakthrough early when Browne played on for 10. Then Chanderpaul and Brian Lara put on a big partnership until Lara made a mistake, but then Richardson joined Chanderpaul and they took the score to about 160 before Chanderpaul went.'

Had bookmakers been fielding on the result at that stage Australia would have been 100-1 to win and the Windies unbackable. But as WC Fields once said: 'It ain't over till the fat lady sings', and although the Australian players could hear her warming up in the wings not a note had been sung.

'Warney started to weave his magic and they started to fall like nine-pins. First Carl Hooper for 2 and then Otis Gibson for 1. Jimmy Adams only lasted a few balls before he was sent packing.

AUSTRALIA v NEW ZEALAND
Madras, India. March 11 1996
(Fourth quarter-final)
Toss: New Zealand. Result: Australia won by 6 wickets

NEW ZEALAND
CM Spearman c Healy b Reiffel	12
NJ Astle c Healy b Fleming	1
LK Germon*† c Fleming b McGrath	89
SP Fleming c SR Waugh b McGrath	8
CZ Harris c Reiffel b Warne	130
RG Twose b Bevan	4
CL Cairns c Reiffel b ME Waugh	4
AC Parore lbw Warne	11
SA Thomson run out	11
DN Patel not out	3
DJ Nash	
Sundries (LB 6, W 3, NB 4)	13
TOTAL (Overs: 50)	9 for 286

F/W 15 16 44 212 227 240 259 283 286

AUSTRALIA
MA Taylor* c Germon b Patel	10
ME Waugh c Parore b Nash	110
RT Ponting c sub (RJ Kennedy) b Thomson	31
SK Warne lbw Astle	24
SR Waugh not out	59
SG Law not out	42
MG Bevan	
IA Healy†	
PR Reiffel	
DW Fleming	
GD McGrath	
Sundries (B 1, LB 6, W 3, NB 3)	13
TOTAL (Overs: 47.5)	4 for 289

F/W 19 84 127 213

Bowler	Ovrs	Mdns	Runs	Wkts	NB	W
AUSTRALIA						
Reiffel	4	0	38	1	—	—
Fleming	5	1	20	1	—	—
McGrath	9	2	50	2	—	—
ME Waugh	8	0	43	1	—	—
Warne	10	0	52	2	—	—
Bevan	10	0	52	1	—	—
SR Waugh	4	0	25	0	—	—

Bowler	Ovrs	Mdns	Runs	Wkts	NB	W
NEW ZEALAND						
Nash	9	1	44	1	—	—
Patel	8	0	45	1	—	—
Cairns	6.5	0	51	0	—	—
Harris	10	0	41	0	—	—
Thomson	8	0	57	1	—	—
Astle	3	0	21	1	—	—
Twose	3	0	23	0	—	—

Punter—First Tests of a Champion

'When Keith Arthurton went for a duck—our spirits were lifted to an all-time high.

'Richardson was trying valiantly to win the game off his own bat by trying to control the strike but they were still too many runs in arrears for that to work.

'Ian Bishop went for 3 and Curtly Ambrose was run out for 2. Richardson was at the non-striker's end on 49 with

AUSTRALIA v WEST INDIES
Chandigarh, India, March 14 1996
(Second semi-final)
Toss: Australia. Result: Australia won by 5 runs

AUSTRALIA
ME Waugh lbw Ambrose	0
MA Taylor* b Bishop	1
RT Ponting lbw Ambrose	0
SR Waugh b Bishop	3
SG Law run out	72
MG Bevan c Richardson b Harper	69
IA Healy† run out	31
PR Reiffel run out	7
SK Warne not out	6
DW Fleming	
GD McGrath	
Sundries (LB 11, W 5, NB 2)	18
TOTAL (Overs: 50)	8 for 207

F/W 0 7 8 15 153 171 186 207

WEST INDIES
S Chanderpaul c Fleming b McGrath	80
CO Browne† c & b Warne	10
BC Lara b SR Waugh	45
RB Richardson* not out	49
RA Harper lbw McGrath	2
OD Gibson c Healy b Warne	1
JC Adams lbw Warne	2
KLT Arthurton c Healy b Fleming	0
IR Bishop lbw Warne	3
CEL Ambrose run out	2
CA Walsh b Fleming	0
Sundries (LB 4, W 2, NB 2)	8
TOTAL (Overs: 49.3)	202

F/W 25 93 165 173 178 183 187 194 202 202

Bowler	Ovrs	Mdns	Runs	Wkts	NB	W
WEST INDIES						
Ambrose	10	1	26	2	—	—
Bishop	10	1	35	2	—	—
Walsh	10	1	33	0	—	—
Gibson	2	0	13	0	—	—
Harper	9	0	47	1	—	—
Adams	9	0	42	0	—	—

Bowler	Ovrs	Mdns	Runs	Wkts	NB	W
AUSTRALIA						
McGrath	10	2	30	2	—	—
Fleming	8.3	0	48	2	—	—
Warne	9	0	36	4	—	—
ME Waugh	4	0	16	0	—	—
SR Waugh	7	0	30	1	—	—
Reiffel	5	0	13	0	—	—
Bevan	4	1	12	0	—	—
Law	2	0	13	0	—	—

the last man in, Courtney Walsh, very much out of form with the bat.

'Then Damien Fleming knocked over Walsh's stumps with the first ball he delivered to him. The feeling we all had at that moment is one we will cherish for the rest of our lives. It was the greatest fightback I have ever been involved with and ever likely to be. We were gone for all money but we never gave up—that is what makes playing for Australia so great.'

The team had been a part of one of the most courageous fightbacks in international one-day history and that night the team partied on until the early hours of the morning.

The stage was set for a thrilling final between Australia and Sri Lanka at Lahore.

With all that had gone on before the tournament began and for the Aussies to be pitted against Sri Lanka, the team that had become its arch rival, made for plenty of media coverage.

Ricky plays it down: 'It was typical of any final with all the players on edge and determined to return home the best one-day side in the world.

'We won the toss and batted but lost Junior for 12 which left me and Tubby to share a decent stand for the first wicket.

'I got out to a pull shot for 45 and then Steve Waugh (13) and Warney (2) had short stays at the crease. Tubby was solid and gave us the good foundation with his 74 and then Stuart Law (22) and Bevo shared a decent stand until "Judge" (Law) departed and Heals went soon after for two.

'We ended up 7 for 241 which we thought might be just enough to scrape home.

'The Sri Lankans lost two early wickets, Jayasuriya (9)

and Kaluwitharana (6), and then they went at us with all guns blazing.

'Asanka Gurinsinha belted 65 in quick time and Aravinda De Silva cut loose, and he and captain Arjuna Ranatunga (47) steered them to an easy victory.

'After the West Indies fightback the final was a real letdown and I know every player in the team felt the pain.'

SRI LANKA v AUSTRALIA
Lahore, Pakistan, March 17 1996
(Final)
Toss: Sri Lanka. Result: Sri Lanka won by 7 wickets

AUSTRALIA
MA Taylor* c Jayasuriya b de Silva	74
ME Waugh c Jayasuriya b Vaas	12
RT Ponting b de Silva	45
SR Waugh c de Silva b Dharmasena	13
SK Warne st Kaluwitharana b Muralitharan	2
SG Law c de Silva b Jayasuriya	22
MG Bevan not out	36
IA Healy*† b de Silva	2
PR Reiffel not out	13
DW Fleming	
GD McGrath	
Sundries (LB 10, NB 1, W 11)	22
TOTAL (Overs: 50)	7 for 241

F/W 36 137 152 156 170 202 205

SRI LANKA
ST Jayasuriya run out	9
RS Kaluwitharana† c Bevan b Fleming	6
AP Gurinsinha b Reiffel	65
PA de Silva not out	107
A Ranatunga* not out	47
HP Tillekeratne	
RS Mahanama	
HPDK Dharmasena	
WPUJC Vaas	
M Muralitharan	
GP Wickremasinghe	
Sundries (B 1, LB 4, W 5, NB 1)	11
TOTAL (Overs: 46.2)	3 for 245

F/W 12 23 148

Bowler SRI LANKA	Ovrs	Mdns	Runs	Wkts	NB	W
Wickremasinghe	7	0	38	0	—	—
Vaas	6	1	30	1	—	—
Muralitharan	10	0	31	1	—	—
Dharmasena	10	0	47	1	—	—
Jayasuriya	8	0	43	1	—	—
de Silva	9	0	42	3	—	—

Bowler AUSTRALIA	Ovrs	Mdns	Runs	Wkts	NB	W
McGrath	8.2	1	28	0	—	—
Fleming	6	0	43	1	—	—
Warne	10	0	58	0	—	—
Reiffel	10	0	49	1	—	—
ME Waugh	6	0	35	0	—	—
SR Waugh	3	0	15	0	—	—
Bevan	3	0	12	0	—	—

Home for a break

At the end of the World Cup Ricky returned home to Tasmania for a well-earned break after what had been a long, hectic, yet wonderful first season as a member of the Australian Test and one-day team. It was time to unwind and catch up with family and friends and ponder what the forthcoming season might bring.

'When I arrived home all I wanted to do was spend some quality time with my girlfriend Kellie and unwind from the tour. I was also looking forward to some home cooking and tucking into some junk food like pizzas, KFC and the odd Big Mac. It's not that I am a junk food freak but we are restricted to a very limited selection of foods on the subcontinent; even the stuff they served up on the flight home was something to look forward to!

'Reflecting back on the season it would have to be my best by far, although I felt as if I hadn't performed as well as I could have in the World Cup. I set myself high standards because that's the only way to succeed at any sport.

'On a personal level, making my Test debut in Perth was a major highlight of my career and batting well enough to almost get a century was very satisfying. My first century (123) in international one-dayers against Sri Lanka was the first time I have ever felt the buzz of a huge Melbourne crowd's cheer and reaching my first ton (102) against the West Indies in the World Cup was another thrill even though that was dampened because we lost the match.

'But from both a personal and team point of view, being part of that incredible win against the Windies to make it into the World Cup final was just unbelievable.

'I'm sure everyone in Australia who watched it on TV

would have got a buzz, but the feeling out there on the ground and in the rooms after the game was absolutely electric. I only wish we hadn't lost the World Cup final the way we did.'

Chapter nine

THE FIRST SEASON

WITH about three months of R&R under his belt, Ricky geared up for what he expected to be his first full season as a regular member of Australia's Test and limited-over teams.

A trip back to Colombo in August in 1996 for the Singer World Series was to mark the start of an extremely long season for the Australians. The controversy over the Australians' refusal to play Sri Lanka in Colombo because of the political unrest and bomb attacks in the central business district of the country's capital only six months prior remained a concern.

'Knowing we were going to Colombo was a bit of a worry to some players but after experiencing first-hand the strict security during the World Cup most of us were more at ease about making the trip.'

Keeping fit

'As usual we all attended training camps prior to the tour and I spent a few hours each day at the gym getting back in shape after putting on a couple of extra kilos during the break.

'I have never been one to pile on the beef but when you are away from the game for three months or more and don't watch the diet as strictly as when you are playing, the body tends to expand a bit in a few places.

'What I try to do is work out in the gym and set up a program that gets me to a certain level of fitness before the season starts until I reach a certain fitness level I am able to at least maintain during the season. If I was just playing Shield and Test cricket it would be easy to stick to a more rigid training program in the gym, but with all the one-day cricket that we play these days it would be impossible to keep up a full fitness program for the whole season. And if I tried, I'm sure I would suffer from burn-out in no time.

'A strict diet also is important when preparing for a season. When we go to the Australian team pre-season training camps a dietitian is there to give us advice on what types of foods will best serve us to keep our bodies in top condition.

'The proper diet usually consists of what the dietitians call performance foods which is primarily plenty of carbohydrates and as little of the fatty foods as possible, which pretty much counts out KFC.

'Beer is not the preferred beverage for a diet but most of the players are partial to a few glasses of the amber fluid after matches—that's something I don't think will ever change!'

* * *

Off to the Singer World Series

'The break had done me the world of good and I felt fresh and looking forward to taking on the Sri Lankans again. There was a lot less hostility in Colombo when we arrived and the security was still strong but we weren't sure how the Sri Lankan crowds would react at the games. A lot of criticism was hurled at us over our decision to forfeit our match against Sri Lanka in the World Cup, especially in the local press. But with Sri Lanka flogging us in the World Cup final I guessed there wouldn't be as much hostility.

'Our first match was against Zimbabwe and we had no trouble winning that and I was pleased with my 53, although their bowling attack was not as sharp as we expected.'

The next game was against Sri Lanka and as expected the crowd was packed into the stadium like a tin of sardines. The stage was set for another classic encounter with Australia having first use of what looked to be a fantastic batting strip.

'I was dropped down the order to number six and when I reached the crease we were well placed to set a target of about 300. I was unbeaten on 46 at the end of our innings and with a total of 280 we were in with a big show.

'But they reached the target for the loss of only six wickets and with a few overs to spare, so we had to eat humble pie again.

'We then went on to defeat India to make it to the final but I played all over the third ball I faced from Joshi and was trapped in front and out for a duck.'

Another loss to the Sri Lankans in a series final would be a very hard pill for the Australian team to swallow, but in a rain-shortened game the home team had little trouble in securing their second world crown in six months, leaving

AUSTRALIA v ZIMBABWE
R. Premadasa (Khettarama) Stadium, Colombo. August 26, 1996
Toss: Australia. Result: Australia won by 125 runs

AUSTRALIA	Runs	Min	Bls	4s	6s
MJ Slater c Strang b Whittall	50	79	70	4	—
ME Waugh b Strang	18	43	26	2	—
RT Ponting c & b Whittall	53	93	82	—	—
SR Waugh c Campbell b Whittall	82	89	69	4	4
SG Law b Streak	20	44	24	1	—
MG Bevan c Campbell b Brandes	9	10	8	1	—
IA Healy*† b Brandes	5	18	10	—	—
GB Hogg not out	11	16	14	—	—
PR Reiffel					
DW Fleming					
GD McGrath					
Sundries (B 1, LB 8, W 3, NB 3)	15				
TOTAL (Overs: 50.0—Mins: 199)	7 for 263				

F/W 48 92 167 230 240 242 263

Bowler	Ovrs	Mdns	Runs	Wkts	NB	W
Streak	10	1	50	1	2	2
Brandes	10	1	47	2	—	1
Strang	9	—	41	1	—	—
GW Flower	6	—	28	—	—	—
Whittall	10	—	53	3	1	—
Dekker	3	—	17	—	—	—
Shah	2	—	18	—	—	—

ZIMBABWE	Runs	Min	Bls	4s	6s
GW Flower c Ponting b Fleming	7	20	23	—	—
AH Shah c ME Waugh b Hogg	41	—	78	—	1
A Flower† lbw Fleming	0	1	2	—	—
ADR Campbell* lbw McGrath	9	20	11	1	—
CB Wishart c Healy b Reiffel	0	7	7	—	—
GJ Whittall b Reiffel	11	34	27	1	—
CN Evans c Healy b SR Waugh	15	29	29	2	—
MH Dekker not out	10	49	42	—	—
PA Strang b ME Waugh	9	28	26	—	—
HH Streak b ME Waugh	0	1	1	—	—
EA Brandes c Hogg b ME Waugh	15	9	13	2	1
Sundries (LB 4, W 10, NB 7)	21				
TOTAL (Overs: 41.0—Mins: 165)	138				

F/W 16 16 33 35 56 98 100 120 120 138

Bowler	Ovrs	Mdns	Runs	Wkts	NB	W
McGrath	7	2	13	1	—	2
Fleming	7	—	24	2	1	3
Reiffel	6	1	23	2	2	—
SR Waugh	7	2	24	1	1	3
Hogg	9	2	26	1	3	2
ME Waugh	5	1	24	3	—	—

Umpires: KT Francis & WAU Wickremasinghe (TV Umpire—CJ Mitchley)
Referee: JR Reid
Man of Match: SR Waugh

SRI LANKA v AUSTRALIA
R. Premadasa (Khettarama) Stadium, Colombo. August 30, 1996
Toss: Australia. Result: Sri Lanka won by four wickets

AUSTRALIA	Runs	Min	Bls	4s	6s
ME Waugh c & b Jayasuriya	50	87	53	7	—
MJ Slater run out (Chandana)	9	24	19	—	—
SG Law c Tillakaratne b Dharmasena	13	12	8	1	—
MG Bevan c Vaas b Chandana	56	44	79	2	—
SR Waugh b Muralitharan	22	45	35	—	—
RT Ponting not out	46	79	57	1	1
DS Lehmann st Kaluwitharana b Chandana	2	14	4	—	—
IA Healy*† c Ranatunga b Muralitharan	8	16	16	—	—
JN Gillespie st Kaluwitharana b Chandana	6	13	13	—	—
DW Fleming c Chandana b Jayasuriya	3	5	6	—	—
GD McGrath not out	8	17	12	—	—
Sundries (LB 3, NB 2)	5				
TOTAL (Overs: 50.0—Mins: 210)	9 for 228				

F/W 21 52 97 149 157 163 178 198 203

Bowler	Ovrs	Mdns	Runs	Wkts	NB	W
Vaas	7	—	29	—	2	—
De Silva	4	—	25	—	1	—
Dharmasena	9	—	49	1	—	—
Muralitharan	10	—	41	2	1	—
Jayasuriya	10	—	43	2	—	—
Chandana	10	—	38	3	—	—

SRI LANKA	Runs	Min	Bls	4s	6s
ST Jayasuriya c Healy b Fleming	44	58	28	8	1
RS Kaluwitharana† b SR Waugh	8	14	13	1	—
AP Gurinsinha run out (Lehmann)	16	38	30	2	—
PA De Silva not out	83	144	95	11	—
A Ranatunga* lbw Fleming	0	4	3	—	—
HP Tillakaratne lbw Fleming	1	10	10	—	—
RS Mahanama b McGrath	50	95	78	3	—
UDU Chandana not out	14	27	24	2	—
HDPK Dharmasena					
WPUJC Vaas					
M Muralitharan					
Sundries (LB 3, W 7, NB 6)	16				
TOTAL (Overs: 45.5—Mins: 198)	6 for 232				

F/W 22 78 78 78 81 196

Bowler	Ovrs	Mdns	Runs	Wkts	NB	W
SR Waugh	5	1	36	1	3	2
Law	2	—	23	—	—	2
McGrath	9.5	—	44	1	4	—
Fleming	8	1	26	3	—	1
Gillespie	6	—	27	—	2	1
Waugh	5	—	29	—	—	—
Lehmann	6	—	26	—	—	—
Bevan	4	—	18	—	—	—

Umpires: SA Bucknor & CJ Mitchley (TV Umpire—BC Cooray)
Referee: JR Reid
Man of Match: PA De Silva

AUSTRALIA v INDIA
Sinhalese Sports Club, Colombo. September 6, 1996
Toss: Australia. Result: Australia won by three wickets

INDIA

	Runs	Min	Bls	4s	6s
NR Mongia† c Bevan b McGrath	38	45	30	8	—
SR Tendulkar* c SR Waugh b McGrath	7	24	11	1	—
RS Dravid b Reiffel	13	45	25	1	—
M Azharuddin c ME Waugh b Reiffel	3	6	6	—	—
VG Kambli c Healy b McGrath	1	7	7	—	—
AD Jadeja c & b SR Waugh	6	30	17	1	—
SC Ganguly lbw Bevan	59	102	75	7	—
SB Joshi b Bevan	48	70	67	5	—
J Srinath run out (Fleming)	2	6	5	—	—
AR Kumble c SR Waugh b ME Waugh	0	9	3	—	—
VBK Prasad not out	6	5	7	—	—
Sundries (LB 3, W 11, NB 4)	18				
TOTAL (Overs: 41.0—Mins: 179)	201				

F/W 32 64 67 68 72 89 189 191 194 201

Bowler	Ovrs	Mdns	Runs	Wkts	NB	W
McGrath	9	1	33	3	2	1
Fleming	6	—	25	—	—	3
Reiffel	5	—	37	2	2	2
SR Waugh	6	—	20	1	—	2
Hogg	5	—	33	—	—	1
ME Waugh	7	—	36	1	—	2
Bevan	3	—	14	2	—	—

AUSTRALIA

	Runs	Min	Bls	4s	6s
MJ Slater c Azharuddin b Prasad	29	75	56	4	—
ME Waugh c Tendulkar b Joshi	23	48	33	3	—
RT Ponting lbw Joshi	0	2	3	—	—
SR Waugh st Mongia b Kumble	55	110	83	2	—
SG Law c Dravid b Prasad	67	80	70	3	2
MG Bevan not out	12	33	9	1	—
IA Healy*† run out (Azharuddin)	4	14	13	—	—
GB Hogg b Kumble	2	10	4	—	—
PR Reiffel not out	1	1	1	—	—
DW Fleming					
GD McGrath					
Sundries (LB 2, W 4, NB 3)	9				
TOTAL (Overs: 44.3—Mins: 190)	7 for 202				

F/W 50 50 69 182 185 194 197

Bowler	Ovrs	Mdns	Runs	Wkts	NB	W
Srinath	6	—	32	—	2	1
Prasad	9	—	53	2	1	2
Joshi	9	1	23	2	—	—
Kumble	8.3	1	36	2	—	—
Tendulkar	8	—	38	—	—	—
Jadeja	4	—	18	—	—	1

Umpires: BC Cooray & KT Francis (TV Umpire—SA Bucknor)
Referee: JR Reid
Man of Match: SR Waugh

the Australians to wander off the field with their tails between their legs.

'They say you have to know how to lose to fully appreciate a victory, but going down without a decent fight in another final to Sri Lanka left a bitter taste in our mouths.'

Australia had seemingly lost its edge at international level but for that miraculous win over the West Indies in a World Cup semi-final six months earlier. Since then the team had made heavy weather of its tasks and the media was beginning to hone in on the bona fides of some individuals in the line-up.

'There was speculation that there was discontent in the Australian camp but that could not have been further from the truth. We were still working well as a team, but we weren't getting the breaks when they counted and subsequently we went through a sort of grey patch.'

A glimmer of hope

With the first mission unaccomplished the Australians then headed to India for a one-off Test against India and a crack at the three-nation Titan Cup. The most often asked question was, could the team pull itself together?

'Despite losing the Singer series final our spirits were still high and we were very optimistic about our chances of success in India,' Ricky says. 'We trained well leading up to the Test in Delhi, although I was starting to struggle a bit in the nets. I felt for the first time in ages that everything was not as it should be. It showed up in the Test because I failed in both innings scoring 14 and 13, and to make

SRI LANKA v AUSTRALIA
Sinhalese Sports Club, Colombo. September 7, 1996
Toss: Australia. Result: Sri Lanka won by 50 runs

SRI LANKA

	Runs	Min	Bls	4s	6s
ST Jayasuriya c Law b McGrath	27	21	20	5	—
RS Kaluwitharana† c & b Lehmann	58	68	45	5	—
AP Gurinsinha c Bevan b McGrath	29	90	46	1	—
PA De Silva not out	75	65	64	2	3
A Ranatunga* not out	39	54	40	1	1

RS Mahanama
HP Tillakaratne
HDPK Dharmasena
UDU Chandana
WPUJC Vaas
M Muralitharan

Sundries (B 1, LB 1, W 2, NB 2) 6
TOTAL (Overs: 35.0—Mins: 147)   3 for 234
F/W 42 104 131

Bowler	Ovrs	Mdns	Runs	Wkts	NB	W
McGrath	7	—	35	2	1	1
Fleming	7	—	53	—	—	—
Reiffel	4	—	43	—	3	1
Lehmann	5	—	29	1	—	—
SR Waugh	7	—	31	—	1	—
ME Waugh	5	—	41	—	—	—

AUSTRALIA

	Runs	Min	Bls	4s	6s
ME Waugh run out (Mahanama)	9	20	12	—	—
MJ Slater c Chandana b Vaas	8	12	6	1	—
RT Ponting c Jayasuriya b Vaas	17	25	26	2	—
SR Waugh c & b Chandana	55	79	53	2	1
SG Law c Muralitharan b Dharmasena	31	45	37	2	—
MG Bevan b Dharmasena	7	25	11	—	—
DS Lehmann st Kaluwitharana b Muralitharan	15	16	13	2	—
IA Healy*† c Muralitharan b Chandana	20	29	20	—	—
PR Reiffel c Mahanama b Chandana	12	23	19	—	—
DW Fleming not out	1	4	1	—	—
GD McGrath c Mahanama b Chandana	0	3	3	—	—

Sundries (LB 3, W 4, NB 2) 9
TOTAL (Overs: 33.0—Mins: 145)   184
F/W 17 26 48 104 129 145 151 183 183 184

Bowler	Ovrs	Mdns	Runs	Wkts	NB	W
Vaas	5	—	23	2	—	—
Gurinsinha	2	—	17	—	—	3
De Silva	3	—	18	—	—	—
Muralitharan	7	—	28	1	2	1
Jayasuriya	5	—	27	—	—	—
Dharmasena	5	—	33	2	—	—
Chandana	6	—	35	4	—	—

Umpires: SA Bucknor & CJ Mitchley
Referee: JR Reid
Man of Match: PA De Silva

Ricky Ponting

INDIA v AUSTRALIA
Feroze Shah Kotla Ground, Delhi. October 10, 11, 12, 14, 1996
Toss: Australia. Result: India won by seven wickets

AUSTRALIA

FIRST INNINGS	RUNS		SECOND INNINGS	RUNS
MJ Slater c & b Kumble	44	(2)	c Azharuddin b Johnson	0
MA Taylor* lbw Prasad	27	(1)	c Rathore b Kapoor	37
RT Ponting b Kapoor	14		b Prasad	13
ME Waugh c Dravid b Joshi	26		c Mongia b Kumble	23
SR Waugh c Mongia b Kapoor	0		not out	67
MG Bevan lbw Joshi	26		c Azharuddin b Kumble	33
IA Healy† b Kumble	17		st Mongia b Kumble	12
GB Hogg c Rathore b Kumble	1		c Rathore b Kumble	4
PR Reiffel c Dravid b Kumble	7		lbw Kumble	6
PE McIntyre not out	6		lbw Prasad	16
GD McGrath run out	6		c Mongia b Prasad	0
Sundries (B 4, LB 3, NB 1)	8		(B 9, LB 6, W 1, NB 7)	23
TOTAL	182		TOTAL	234
F/W 47 81 93 94 143 144 147 169 170 182			F/W 4 25 72 78 145 159 171 191 232 234	

Bowler	Ovrs	Mdns	Runs	Wkts	NB	W
FIRST INNINGS						
Prasad	12	4	34	1	—	—
Johnson	4	1	12	—	—	—
Joshi	23	7	36	2	—	—
Kumble	24	7	63	4	—	—
Kapoor	10	3	30	2	—	—
SECOND INNINGS						
Prasad	13.3	7	18	3	—	—
Johnson	12	2	40	1	—	—
Kumble	41	12	67	5	—	—
Joshi	20	7	52	—	—	—
Kapoor	22	5	42	1	—	—

INDIA

FIRST INNINGS	RUNS		SECOND INNINGS	RUNS
VS Rathore c Ponting b Reiffel	5		b Reiffel	14
NR Mongia† b Reiffel	152		lbw Reiffel	0
SC Ganguly c ME Waugh b Hogg	66		not out	21
SR Tendulkar* c ME Waugh b McIntyre	10		b McGrath	0
M Azharuddin b McGrath	17		not out	21
RS Dravid c Healy b SR Waugh	40			
SB Joshi c Ponting b McIntyre	23			
AR Kapoor c Ponting b ME Waugh	22			
AR Kumble lbw Reiffel	2			
D Johnson not out	0			
VBK Prasad b McIntyre	3			
Sundries (B 10, LB 1, NB 10)	21		Sundries (W 1, NB 1)	2
TOTAL	361		TOTAL	3 for 58
F/W 13 144 169 199 260 303 341 353 354 361			F/W 1 25 26	

99

Bowler	Ovrs	Mdns	Runs	Wkts	NB	W
FIRST INNINGS						
McGrath	29	10	56	1	—	—
Reiffel	17	7	35	3	—	—
SR Waugh	13	5	25	1	—	—
McIntyre	37.4	7	103	3	—	—
Hogg	17	3	69	1	—	—
ME Waugh	18	—	62	1	—	—
SECOND INNINGS						
McGrath	7	2	30	1	—	—
Reiffel	6	2	24	2	—	—
McIntyre	0.2	—	4	—	—	—

Umpires: S Venkataraghavan & P Willey

matters worse we lost the match by seven wickets. I walked away from the match with some uncertainty about my form and it was noticed by the selectors.

'Then in the first game of the Titan Cup I struggled to make 35 against South Africa. We lost this game and then I was dropped for the game against India which we also lost.

'I was back in the team for the second crack at South Africa. However, that was another double whammy because I got to 17 before nicking one to the keeper off Pat Symcox and we also suffered our fourth loss on the trot.

'I finished the series the worst way possible with a first-ball duck clean bowled by Boje. That left me with a bit to think about when we got back to Australia.'

Dropped!

Three days before the 1996 Boxing Day Test against the West Indies, Ricky received a call from 'Mr Doom', Australian selector Trevor Hohns.

'I was lying in bed when the phone rang and it was

AUSTRALIA v SOUTH AFRICA
Nehru Stadium, Indore. October 19, 1996
Toss: Australia. Result: South Africa won by seven wickets

AUSTRALIA	Runs	Min	Bls	4s	6s
MA Taylor* run out (Crookes)	39	80	58	3	—
ME Waugh run out (Rhodes)	50	93	68	5	—
RT Ponting c Richardson b Donald	35	80	51	1	—
SR Waugh st Richardson b Symcox	1	7	9	—	—
SG Law c & b Crookes	1	1	2	—	—
MG Bevan b Donald	56	90	76	6	—
IA Healy† c Rhodes b Donald	11	21	24	—	—
GB Hogg not out	11	18	15	—	—
PR Reiffel not out	6	8	5	1	—
JN Gillespie					
GD McGrath					
Sundries (LB 4, W 1, NB 4)	9				
TOTAL (Overs: 50.0—Mins: 202)	7 for 219				

F/W 85 99 103 106 167 197 204

Bowler	Ovrs	Mdns	Runs	Wkts	NB	W
De Villiers	10	—	38	—	1	—
McMillan	9	—	48	—	—	—
Donald	10	—	57	3	3	—
Crookes	10	—	39	1	—	1
Symcox	10	—	28	1	—	—
Cronje	1	—	5	—	—	—

SOUTH AFRICA	Runs	Min	Bls	4s	6s
AC Hudson c Taylor b McGrath	53	103	72	7	—
G Kirsten not out	105	203	134	9	—
DJ Cullinan b McGrath	0	8	6	—	—
WJ Cronje* c Healy b Gillespie	14	41	29	—	—
JN Rhodes not out	19	48	35	1	—
BM McMillan					
PL Symcox					
DJ Richardson†					
DN Crookes					
PS De Villiers					
AA Donald					
Sundries (B 5, LB 14, W 3, NB 7)	29				
TOTAL (Overs: 46.1—Mins: 203)	3 for 220				

F/W 118 129 175

Bowler	Ovrs	Mdns	Runs	Wkts	NB	W
McGrath	10	1	42	2	3	2
Reiffel	10	1	34	—	0	—
Gillespie	10	—	51	1	1	1
Hogg	7.1	—	37	—	—	—
Law	6	—	23	—	—	—
ME Waugh	3	—	14	—	—	—

Umpires: S Banerjee & S Deo (TV Umpire—N Menon)
Referee: JR Reid
12th Man: MJ Slater (Australia)
Man of Match: G Kirsten

Punter—First Tests of a Champion

AUSTRALIA v SOUTH AFRICA
Nahar Singh Stadium, Faridabad. October 25, 1996
Toss: Australia. Result: South Africa won by two wickets

AUSTRALIA	Runs	Min	Bls	4s	6s
MA Taylor* c McMillan b Symcox	42	105	74	3	—
ME Waugh c Richardson b McMillan	16	39	34	2	—
RT Ponting st Richardson b Symcox	17	38	28	2	—
SR Waugh c McMillan b Boje	40	62	60	3	—
MG Bevan c Hudson b Boje	12	14	15	—	—
SG Law run out (Richardson)	52	68	51	4	—
AC Gilchrist† b Donald	18	36	22	1	—
GB Hogg lbw Donald	0	1	1	—	—
PR Reiffel b Donald	0	2	2	—	—
DW Fleming not out	1	9	1	—	—
GD McGrath c Cronje b Donald	1	3	5	—	—
Sundries (B 1, LB 8, W 3, NB 4)	16				
TOTAL (Overs: 47.3—Mins: 193)	215				

F/W 34 72 107 128 162 212 212 212 214 215

Bowler	Ovrs	Mdns	Runs	Wkts	NB	W
De Villiers	9	—	35	—	2	—
McMillan	9	—	41	1	2	—
Cronje	2	—	12	—	—	1
Donald	8.3	—	31	4	—	—
Symcox	10	—	43	2	—	2
Boje	9	—	44	2	—	—

SOUTH AFRICA	Runs	Min	Bls	4s	6s
AC Hudson run out (Waugh, ME)	32	69	45	5	—
G Kirsten b Fleming	1	11	5	—	—
PL Symcox c Bevan b Reiffel	26	23	21	5	—
DJ Cullinan not out	71	163	115	6	—
JN Rhodes b Reiffel	42	116	50	5	—
WJ Cronje* c Gilchrist b Reiffel	0	2	1	—	—
BM McMillan run out (Bevan–Gilchrist)	21	40	32	3	—
DJ Richardson† c Gilchrist b Reiffel	5	13	6	1	—
N Boje c SR Waugh b Hogg	6	10	12	1	—
PS De Villiers not out	0	3	0	—	—
AA Donald					
Sundries (LB 9, W 3, NB 2)	14				
TOTAL (Overs: 47.2—Mins: 196) 8 for 218					

F/W 3 40 77 142 142 184 205 214

Bowler	Ovrs	Mdns	Runs	Wkts	NB	W
Fleming	8.2	1	53	1	—	1
Reiffel	10	—	35	4	—	—
Hogg	8	1	23	1	—	1
McGrath	10	1	50	—	2	—
Law	3	—	14	—	—	—
ME Waugh	8	1	34	—	—	1

Umpires: BA Jamula & MR Singh (TV Umpire—Suresh Shastri)
Referee: JR Reid
12th Man: MJ Slater (Australia)
Man of Match: AA Donald

AUSTRALIA v SOUTH AFRICA
Nehru Stadium, Guwahati. November 1, 1996
Toss: Australia. Result: South Africa won by eight wickets

AUSTRALIA	Runs	Min	Bls	4s	6s
MA Taylor* c Rhodes b Symcox	38	100	78	2	—
SG Law c Cullinan b Klusener	22	30	17	4	—
SR Waugh c McMillan b Boje	37	87	67	1	—
MG Bevan c Symcox b Donald	79	99	95	7	—
RT Ponting b Boje	0	1	1	—	—
MJ Slater not out	53	84	69	4	—
AC Gilchrist† run out (Cronje)	0	1	1	—	—
GB Hogg not out	0	1	0	—	—
PR Reiffel					
DW Fleming					
GD McGrath					
Sundries (LB 7, W 2)	9				
TOTAL (Overs: 50.3—Mins: 205)	6 for 238				

F/W 38 94 113 113 237 237

Bowler	Ovrs	Mdns	Runs	Wkts	NB	W
McMillan	10	2	35	—	—	—
Symcox	10	—	32	1	—	1
Klusener	7	—	55	1	—	—
Donald	9	—	47	1	—	1
Boje	10	—	43	2	—	—
Cronje	4	—	19	—	—	—

SOUTH AFRICA	Runs	Min	Bls	4s	6s
AC Hudson c Hogg b Law	68	110	84	6	—
G Kirsten b Hogg	27	50	34	5	—
L Klusener not out	88	144	99	8	—
DJ Cullinan not out	43	85	64	2	—
WJ Cronje*					
JN Rhodes					
DJ Richardson†					
PL Symcox					
N Boje					
BM McMillan					
AA Donald					
Sundries (LB 1, W 4, NB 8)	13				
TOTAL (Overs: 45.0—Mins: 195)	2 for 239				

F/W 60 133

Bowler	Ovrs	Mdns	Runs	Wkts	NB	W
Fleming	7	—	37	—	—	1
Reiffel	10	1	51	—	5	—
Hogg	8	—	42	1	1	2
McGrath	6	—	41	—	2	—
Waugh	4	—	24	—	—	—
Law	10	—	43	1	—	1

Umpires: K Murali & K Parthasarathy (TV Umpire—S Banerjee)
Referee: JR Reid
12th Man: JN Gillespie (Australia)
Man of Match: PL Symcox

Trevor Hohns. It's common knowledge among the players that the only time you ever hear from Trevor is when you've been dropped. So before he could spurt it out I knew I had been dropped from the team.

'I was shocked because even though my three innings leading up to the Boxing Day Test weren't good I didn't think they would cut me from the team. Trevor told me that I should go back to Shield cricket and sort a few things out and make sure I scored a hell of a lot of runs.'

Ricky's parents were sure he would take the news badly and were there to console him in his hour of need. They dragged him off to the golf course which they hoped would serve as a relaxant as well as shield their son from the media frenzy.

The exercise failed on both counts.

'I was happy to be with Mum and Dad and walking around the golf course at least got me out of the house, but I couldn't quite get my thoughts off being axed. And when we got to the ninth green the media were there in force.

'Tassie is a small place and I should have guessed it wouldn't take the media long to find out where I was.

'The interviews went well and most of the journos were sympathetic. I didn't feel too bad about their questions when they had all gone. But that empty feeling is hopefully something I don't ever have to experience again.

'There were suggestions that it was something other than my form which resulted in me being dropped but that wasn't the case. It wasn't so much my performance in the Tests against the West Indies but more the form I showed in the tour of India.

'I only got 14 and 13 in the one-off Test in India and my one-day efforts weren't anything to write home about.

I knew then that my form was well below what it should have been.

'I stuck my hand up for the number three batting spot and a lot of people said I was sounding my own death knell by trying to occupy the toughest spot in the order, but I believed I could do it. In hindsight it was probably a mistake and I should have been less impetuous and I probably would have settled in to a number six spot, but that's not the way I play the game on the field. I didn't want to hold back from what I believed in. It all boiled down to my loss of form and it wouldn't have mattered where I batted it probably would have been the same result.

'I got bowled a lot on the tour of India and I don't usually get bowled. It was just a case of a few things going wrong and I was just hoping everything would come right when we got back to Australia.

'I hit a few runs in Brisbane against the West Indies with an 88 in the first innings of the First Test but failed in the second. Then I got out to a couple of very average shots in the Sydney Test—that is what obviously cost me my place.

'Once I was told I was dropped it took a while for it to sink in, but once I accepted it I set about doing just what Trevor Hohns had suggested—I went back to Shield cricket to rebuild my confidence.'

There were a lot of people who thought Ricky was harshly treated but he knew deep down that his form wasn't up to scratch. In fact it was well below his capabilities and with other players such as Justin Langer making runs all over the place it was only a matter of time before something happened.

As he says: 'While I was shocked at being dumped it was

more the disappointment in myself which made it so hard to accept.

'A lot of things go through your mind when you have been axed from the Test team because with so many good players waiting in the wings you never really know whether you'll get another chance. I had never been in that situation before and I didn't know how I was going to handle it. One day I had the world at my feet and then the next I had everything taken away from me. It isn't easy coming to terms with that when all you ever wanted to do was play Test cricket and some people only ever get one chance. I guess for a moment I thought I had blown it.'

The general consensus was that Ricky had been led to the slaughter by being thrown into the number three spot in the order, replacing David Boon who had retired from international cricket with the reputation as one of the best number three batters to play for Australia in the past four decades.

'I never pushed for the number three spot initially, although I did say I wanted to bat in that spot when asked by the senior players and selectors.

'Boonie told me that he would like to see me bat down the order for the first couple of years at Test level, but I felt because I had batted at number four nearly all the time for Tassie in the Shield that I was good enough to bat in the number three spot for Australia. In the end I guess I just wasn't good enough at the time.'

The comeback trail was not an easy road to travel for a batsman who had been hailed by former Australian Test captain and prominent cricket commentator Richie Benaud as one of the most promising young strokemakers to play Test cricket since Neil Harvey. Even Shield cricket was presenting problems.

'The big problem was I didn't have a clue what I was doing wrong. This game is like most ball sports where success is very much dependent on confidence. When that falls away you are in trouble.

'It is nothing strange to have a bad run for a couple of games but previously when I had failed to score in a couple of games I would pull it together and make a big score and my form would hold. But my slump had lasted for so long I started to doubt myself.

'I probably tried a bit too hard and made things happen too quickly in my first couple of Shield games back, because I got bugger-all in my first game back against WA at Bellerive and I got 30-odd in Sydney in the next game, but I was still struggling and I had no idea how to get out of the slump.

'But after a few games things started to fall into place and I was finding the middle more often and my confidence grew.

'I relied a lot on State coach Greg Shipperd and he was an enormous help to me during that rough period. I spent more time than normal in the nets working on technique and doing things to help me focus and Shippy was able to sort a few things out with me and the recovery process was in place.

'Finally I strung together three centuries at Bellerive and I felt then I had fully recaptured the form which put me into the Test team in the first place.

'Although it was my 26 in the first innings against Victoria in Melbourne that started to turn things my way. I went out with the intention of batting all day and felt really focused then I started to hit it in the middle of the bat and I could feel my confidence growing. I got out to a very good ball from Tony Dodemaide which cut back sharply taking a faint edge through to the keeper. I was disappointed but I felt as if I could have gone on to make a hundred so it was a real turning point for me. I made 94 not out in the second innings. There were good signs that my timing was back.'

However, Ricky failed in four subsequent visits to the crease before striking top form against South Australia at Bellerive. He belted 126 off a strong attack in Tasmania's first innings of 248 which left no doubt in his mind that the magic had returned.

'The clash with SA was an important game for Tassie because a win would put us into second spot and in with a chance to make the final.

'We trailed by over 100 on the first innings but SA captain Jamie Siddon's declaration in their second dig, which gave them a lead of almost 350, set the scene for a great finish, provided we were up to the task.

'We lost two early wickets and when I went in at 2 for 50 it was do or die as far as I was concerned. I had a lucky escape early on when I was nearly run out and a few runs later I was dropped at silly mid-off.

'Jamie Cox was batting well and we put on a 70-run partnership for the third wicket and then Boonie joined me and we put on 70 odd in quick time.'

When play started that day a paltry crowd of 300 was scattered around the picturesque Bellerive oval but when the word spread that Ricky was on the rampage and looked set to steer Tassie to a remarkable victory, the crowd swelled to over 3000.

Daniel Marsh joined Ricky at the crease. By this time Ricky had reached his century and with Marsh in great form, the pair guided Tasmania to victory with Ricky unbeaten on 145 and Marsh a masterly 49 off only 28 balls.

'Winning the game was far more important to me than getting back-to-back centuries and the beauty of the win was that every player contributed.'

Then Ricky made it three centuries on the trot when he crafted a brilliant 159 in the first innings against Queensland at Bellerive.

'I was hoping the three centuries would convince selectors to give me a berth in the squad to tour England. Thankfully they had faith in me and I got the nod.'

Chapter ten

THE ASHES TOUR OF ENGLAND

BEING back in the Australian team was a relief for Ricky but he had to earn his place in the Test XI. He knew it would not be a walk-up start and he was prepared to spend time carrying the drinks and being a spectator.

'Being a player on the outer was not something new to me because I had experienced it on my first tour to the West Indies in 1995. But having been a regular member of the Australian side and experienced Test cricket, the situation I found myself in on my return to the team was new to me. I never realised how frustrating that could be. You feel a part of the team just because you're there and the mateship and everything else is the same, but when you arrive at the ground on the morning of a game and you know you're not playing it's bloody tough. It's very hard to get excited about the game, but you still do everything you can to help the team prepare for the day's play.

'I went out for practice each day and did all the things I had to do like throw balls to the batters and that sort of stuff, but often when it came my turn to have a hit there was nobody left so I missed out. But I guess that's just part of the learning curve and for some it probably makes them more frustrated and want to give up and with others it makes them more determined to get back in the mainstream of things and that's the approach I took.'

Ricky spent the first three weeks of the tour on the sidelines. In his first game, a one-dayer against Nottingham, he made only 19 but he knew there was a chance of him reclaiming a Test berth if he could craft a big score before the Test against England at Leeds. He got a sniff that there was a chance he could get back into the Test team when Michael Bevan was starting to get sorted out with a few short ones and there looked like there was going to be an opening at number six.

But it was against Glamorgan at Cardiff that Ricky showed the first real glimpse of the form that would earn him a berth in the Test XI.

'I knew that the match against Glamorgan was my chance to get back into the team. I struggled for the first 25 runs or so but that was probably because I put a bit too much pressure on myself, but I struck a couple of straight drives right in the middle that lifted my confidence and I went on to make 126 not out.

'I made 26 not out in the second innings and that really set me up for a berth in the Leeds Test.'

Despite making a modest five against Middlesex at Lord's in the subsequent three-day match, Ricky was selected to play in the Leeds Test, taking over the number six spot in the batting order.

* * *

Handling the pressure

Ricky says there is nothing like pressure to make or break you. 'Pressure is a funny thing because it can work for you and work very much against you, the secret is knowing how to handle it. Greg Blewett is a prime example of what the pressure of holding onto your place in the team can do to your form.

'Greg had a bad time in the Tests in India in 1998 and after we played the last Test over there I had a long talk to him. I could see in him exactly what I was feeling before I was dropped.

'Greg had been dropped before and he knew how hard it was to get back into the team and he was worried about his chances of being able to play his way back into the Test team a second time. I hope he does get back in because he is a marvellous batsman and an ideal number three but it will depend on how he comes to terms with the situation as to whether he plays Test cricket again.

'There are a lot of very talented young players out there champing at the bit to get into the Australian team so there is always some sort of pressure on the players to perform. I know when I set my sights on playing Test cricket I could see some of the players losing form and it made me more determined to score well in Shield games so that my name would be high on the list if an opening came.

'Once I made it into the team and got over the initial excitement of playing Test cricket, although the buzz has never really left me, there was a period when I felt super comfortable. That is a fantastic zone to be in. Your confidence is way up, your self esteem is at an all-time high and you feel as if you can make a century every time you walk to the crease.'

The recurring dream

When Ricky was a child he had dreams about making centuries for Australia at the MCG, hitting the run to win the Ashes series against England and taking the catch of the season to give Tasmania its first Sheffield Shield victory.

But one dream which has developed into a recurring nightmare is the one which gave him a sleepless night in January, 1993.

'I was batting for Tassie against NSW at the SCG in my first season of Shield cricket and I was 98 not out at the end of the day's play. I was poised to make my maiden first-class century and when I finally nodded off to sleep I dreamt that I was run out going for a sharp single to bring up my century.

'That didn't eventuate, luckily I went on to make 135 the next day, but that same dream and others like it have taunted me ever since. I have spoken to other players and they tell me it is common but that doesn't make it any easier.

'I also dream of dropping the simplest of catches which would win Australia an Ashes series. The dreams are always in slow motion and they keep flashing up like a video replay.

'I am not conscious of the dreams when I am on the field but the fact that they have continued for so long is annoying. When I was a kid I used to dream of making centuries every time I went out to bat. I just wish I could start having those type of dreams again.'

* * *

Ashes Test debut

If Ricky could find 'the zone' in his return to the Test arena at Headingly there was little doubt the plucky young Tasmanian would prove his worth.

Australia performed well in the field and Jason Gillespie produced a personal best to have the Poms warming up for their stint in the field with a modest tally of 172 on the board.

Now that Ricky had relinquished the position of first drop his name nestled more comfortably on the scoreboard at the number six spot. But no sooner had the Aussie innings started, Ricky found himself out in the middle with the side reeling at 4 for 50.

'It was not the start we had hoped for and with so much riding on a good performance as far as my career was concerned, the situation the team was in added to the pressure.

'We had lost Tubby, Junior and Blewey cheaply and when I came in to replace Tugga only Herb [Elliott] and I stood between a decent total and trailing by heaps on the first innings.

'I started slowly and cautiously, not so much that I was nervous but because of the position the team was in. It was imperative that Matty and I stick it out for the rest of the day.

'I played a pull shot and struck it so sweetly it rocketed to the boundary. It was like a lead weight had lifted from my shoulders. It is amazing how just one shot can switch you into another gear and frame of mind. Matty was batting well and we started to have some fun, which was something I hadn't been having too much of on the Tour.

'At the close of play I had 84, Matty had reached his ton

Punter—First Tests of a Champion

AUSTRALIA v ENGLAND
Headingsly, Leeds. July 24-28, 1997
Toss: Australia. Result: Australia won by an innings and 61 runs

ENGLAND

FIRST INNINGS	RUNS	SECOND INNINGS	RUNS
MA Butcher c Blewett b Reiffel	24	c Healy b McGrath	19
MA Atherton* c Gillespie b McGrath	41	c Warne b McGrath	2
AJ Stewart† c Blewett b Gillespie	7	b Reiffel	16
N Hussain c Taylor b McGrath	26	c Gillespie b Warne	105
DW Headley c SR Waugh b Gillespie	22	GP Thorpe c ME Waugh b Gillespie	15
GP Thorpe b Gillespie	15	JP Crawley b Reiffel	72
JP Crawley c Blewett b Gillespie	2	MA Ealham c ME Waugh b Reiffel	4
MA Ealham not out	8	DW Headey lbw b Reiffel	3
RDB Croft c Ponting b Gillespie	6	c Healy b Reiffel	5
D Gough b Gillespie	0	c ME Waugh b Gillespie	0
AM Smith b Gillespie	0	not out	4
Sundries (B 4, LB 4, W 1, NB 12)	21	(B 6, LB 4, NB 13)	23
TOTAL (Overs: 59.4)	All out for 72	TOTAL (Overs: 91.1)	All out for 268

F/W 43 58 103 138 154 154 163 172 172 172

F/W 23 28 57 89 222 252 256 263 264 268

Bowler	Ovrs	Mdns	Runs	Wkts	NB	W
FIRST INNINGS						
McGrath	22	5	67	2	2	1
Reiffel	20	4	41	1	10	—
Gillespie	13.4	1	37	7	—	—
Blewett	3	0	17	0	—	—
Warne	1	0	2	0	—	—
SECOND INNINGS						
McGrath	22	5	80	2	2	—
Reiffel	21.1	2	49	5	6	—
Gillespie	23	8	65	2	2	—
Warne	21	6	53	1	2	—
SR Waugh	4	1	11	0	1	—

AUSTRALIA

FIRST INNINGS	RUNS
MA Taylor* c Stewart b Gough	0
MTG Elliott b Gough	199
GS Blewett c Stewart b Gough	1
ME Waugh c & b Headley	8
SR Waugh c Crawley b Headley	4
RT Ponting c Ealham b Gough	127
IA Healy† b Ealham	31
SK Warne c Thorpe b Ealham	0
PR Reiffel not out	54
JN Gillespie b Gough	3
GD McGrath not out	20
Sundries (B 9, LB 10, NB 35)	54
TOTAL (Overs: 123)	9 dec 501

FW 0 16 43 50 318 382 383 444 461

Bowler	Ovrs	Mdns	Runs	Wkts	NB	W
FIRST INNINGS						
Gough	36	5	149	5	8	—
Headley	25	2	125	2	12	—
Smith	23	2	89	0	7	—
Ealham	19	3	56	2	2	—
Croft	18	1	49	0	—	—
Butcher	2	0	14	0	6	—

Umpires: MJ Kitchen and CJ Mitchley (South Africa)
Third Umpire: R. Julian
Match Referee: CW Smith (West Indies)
Man of Match: JN Gillespie

and we had taken a handy first innings lead—all in all a good day's work.

'I felt good when I walked off the ground and I was looking forward to getting back out there the next day to finish off the job. I had a really good night's sleep, no dreams about being run out on 99, and walked to the crease the next morning feeling on top of the world.

'I brought up my ton without too much fuss, turning one down the leg side and then charged off for the single. I think I nearly pulled my arm out of its socket when I punched the air with the bat because there is nothing like scoring a century in Test cricket, especially when it is your first.

'I had mixed emotions because I felt as if I had answered my critics, done a great job for my country and was also relieved to finally score a ton at Test level.

'It definitely made up for me just missing out on my Test debut against Sri Lanka but more importantly it renewed my self belief. I got out on 127, although I felt like I could have batted forever, but it was probably the best innings of my career.'

A young Ponting accepts his awards for topping batting aggregates and averages, most promising player and best individual performance for his centuries in each innings for Tasmania in the Shield game against WA.
　　　　　　　　　　Courtesy of Kim Eiszele and *The Mercury, Hobart*

Above: Ricky out for 1 bowled by Brad McNamara. Not a good day for Punter or Tasmania in the Sheffield Shield final at the SCG in 1994.
　　　Courtesy of Chris Crerar and
　　　　　　　The Mercury, Hobart

Left: Ricky and his dad spend some quality time together on the golf course.
　Courtesy of Drew Fitzgibbon and
　　　　　The Mercury, Hobart

At home there are always a few chores to be done.
Courtesy of Drew Fitzgibbon and *The Mercury, Hobart*

Above: Ricky and David Boon on board the Seaflight Ferry on their way out for an evening cruise on Auckland's Waitemata Harbour during a break on the 1995 tour of New Zealand.
Courtesy of G. Jeffrey and NZ Herald

Right: Punter lofts one into the deep during a game of beach cricket in Bermuda at the end of the West Indies tour in 1995.
Courtesy of Ben Radford and Allsport

Above: Lorraine Ponting at the NTCA ground only moments after Ricky is named in the Test team.
Courtesy of Drew Fitzgibbon and *The Mercury, Hobart*

Left: Ricky always has time to sign autographs for kids. Here he signs a bat for three of his fans.
Courtesy of Barry Winburn and *The Mercury, Hobart*

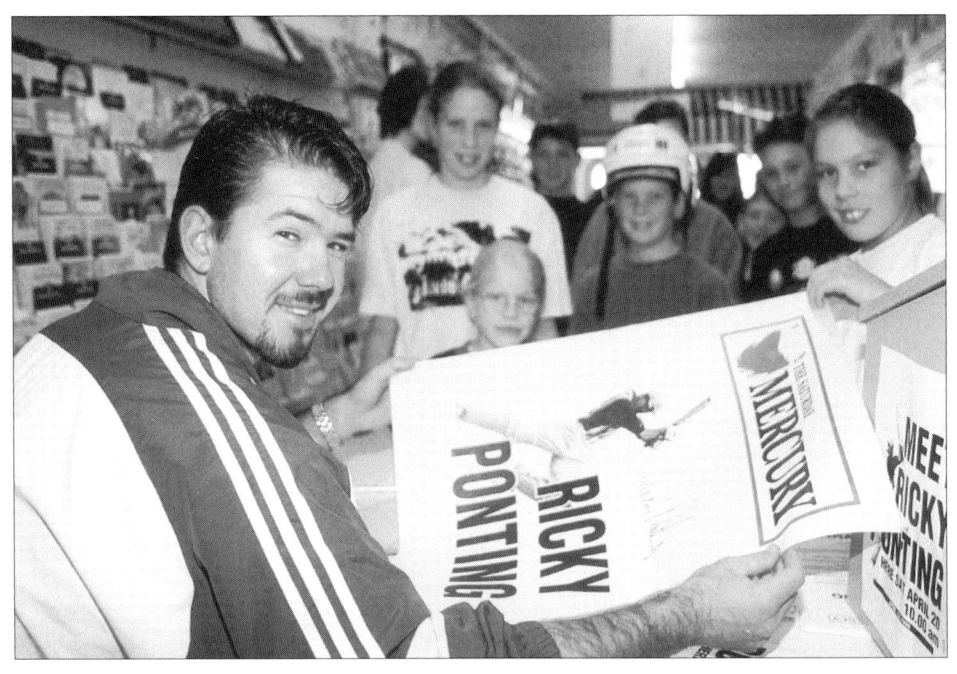

Above: Working with sponsors is just part of the job. Here Ricky signs posters in a Hobart newsagency. Courtesy of Fred Kohl and *The Mercury, Hobart*

Below: Ricky and his girlfriend Kellie Sainty embrace after a Shield game at Bellerive. Courtesy of Drew Fitzgibbon and *The Mercury, Hobart*

Above: Ricky is as adept with the keeper's gloves as he is with the bat.
Courtesy of Drew Fitzgibbon and *The Mercury, Hobart*

Left: Ponting square drives a ball during the one-day final for Australia v Sri Lanka at the MCG in 1996.
Courtesy of Joe Mann and Allsport

Above: In the swing. Apart from his prowess with the bat, Ricky Ponting is also a talented golfer.
Courtesy of Raoul Kochanowski and *The Mercury, Hobart*

Right: Ricky with his younger brother Drew clowning around at the Mowbray Golf Club.
Courtesy of Drew Fitzgibbon and *The Mercury, Hobart*

Left: The day in December 1996 that Ricky was dropped from the Australian Test team. He headed for some peace on the golf course with his mum, but his mobile phone ran hot.

Courtesy of Drew Fitzgibbon and
The Mercury, Hobart

Below: Ricky Ponting shows his form with the ball in the Mercantile Mutual Cup.

Courtesy of James Kerr and
The Mercury, Hobart

Left: At Bellerive Oval Ricky raises his bat to the grandstand on his ton.
    Courtesy of James Kerr and *The Mercury, Hobart*

Below: Jamie Cox and Ricky cool off during a drinks break on their way to a record partnership for Tasmania in February 1997.
    Courtesy of James Kerr and *The Mercury, Hobart*

Ricky (left) and Jamie Cox are good mates on and off the field. Here he congratulates Jamie on reaching 1000 first-class runs for the season.
Courtesy of James Kerr and *The Mercury, Hobart*

Above: Ricky gathers a selection of bats for his first Test tour of England.
Courtesy of Drew Fitzgibbon and The Mercury, Hobart.

Right: Another Ponting boundary resulting from a powerful pull shot.
Courtesy of Ben Radford and Allsport

Ponting makes a powerful and elegant drive during the Fourth Test at Leeds in 1997. Courtesy of Clive Mason and Allsport

A Ponting square drive finds the boundary during the Second Test at the SCG in 1998. Courtesy of Ben Radford and Allsport.

Ricky hooks one over the square leg boundary in a World Series Cup for Australia-A v New Zealand at the MCG. Courtesy of Ben Radford and Allsport

Above: Ricky sets off for a quick single after guiding one through the gully.
Courtesy of Shaun Botterill and Allsport

Right: A confident and excited Ricky 'Punter' Ponting on the eve of his departure for the Commonwealth Games and then Pakistan with the Australian Test team in August 1998.
Courtesy of Peter Aitchison

Part two

The Game

Chapter eleven

THE PRESSURES OF AN INTERNATIONAL GAME

THE media play an important role in sport in Australia and knowing how to handle the written word and opinions of electronic media commentators is becoming more and more a part of a cricketer's armour. However, Ricky has always had a good relationship with the media and he realised very early in his career that good press can assist a player in his quest to play at the highest level.

'When I was dropped from the Test team the journos, in general, thought I had been harshly treated and they looked after me a bit but in contrast when Matthew Elliott was dropped he opted to shun the media—all that did was give them more bullets to fire at him,' Ricky says. 'The important thing is to try and work with the media and as long as they respect your private life and concentrate on cricket matters there is never a problem as far as I'm concerned. However, I think the British tabloids are not worth the paper they are printed on. I wonder how some of the journos who work in that environment can sleep peacefully at night. In contrast most of the TV commentators in Australia are former great Test cricketers and that makes them well qualified to make certain comments about players. For example, Bill Lawry can be a bit of a wally the way he carries on sometimes but he has a wonderful knowledge of the game. He wouldn't have been captain of Australia and been so successful if he wasn't one of the best of his era. However, the players don't have a lot to do with the TV commentators; we mainly deal with the newspaper scribes. Most of them have a fairly good understanding of the game, but other than match reports, journos are usually on the lookout for a negative story but I guess that is what sells more papers.'

When Ricky was on the verge of making his Test debut he was contracted as a columnist with the *Hobart Mercury*, with his regular column usually co-written by one of the nation's top cricket scribes, David Stockdale.

'I was apprehensive about doing a column in the local newspaper, mainly because I thought people might determine it as a bit of an ego trip,' Ricky says. 'But after a while it sat more comfortably with me and hopefully it is good value for the newspaper.'

Making the headlines

During the 1998 tour of India Ricky was involved in an incident in a nightclub which sent the media into a feeding frenzy and the aftermath had the potential to ruin his career. The incident made headlines worldwide and even in Australia the newspapers were at their tabloid best.

An attractive woman allegedly claimed Ricky had accosted her in the nightclub and that her companion had come to her aid resulting in an altercation between Ricky and the woman's male companion. There were calls for a police investigation and all of a sudden Ricky's career was in jeopardy but what really happened in the nightclub that night was never reported.

'A few of the players wanted to go to a nightspot and so this guy had organised for us to get into a nightclub in Calcutta that was usually restricted to members and special guests,' Ricky says. 'When we arrived at the nightclub this same guy spoke to the doorman. He explained we were Australian cricketers and after a few minutes, they let us in.

'What we didn't know was that it was a couples night which meant the only way men could get in was in the company of a female. We were quite happy just hanging out together and having a few drinks, and for me it was a chance to celebrate North Melbourne's win in the AFL Ansett Cup final in Melbourne.'

Ricky's beloved Kangaroos had scored a convincing win over St Kilda in the final of the pre-season championship at the MCG, which many of the Australian players watched on cable TV.

'Everyone was having a good time and knocking down a few beers and the next thing I knew I was asked to leave by one of the security guys. I am usually the last one to leave a nightclub and I wanted to stay, and there was a scuffle but that is all there was to it. I didn't realise we were the only single guys there.

'To be honest I couldn't remember half of what went on during the night because I'd had a skinful but I definitely did not assault a woman in the nightclub. Thankfully I had enough witnesses to prove it.

'But the media had a field day and some of the things

that were written in the papers made it difficult for me to get a grasp on the situation and I was hauled up before tour management to give them my side of the story.

'After my meeting with tour management I was handed a press release to read to the media as it was the intention of management to clear the matter up as quickly as we could.'

The nightclub incident had a devastating effect on Ricky who described the aftermath as one of the most traumatic times in his sporting career.

'When the story appeared in the newspapers in India I knew it would be the same back in Australia, and when I saw what the Australian media had done with the story I was horrified. Even though I had done nothing like what the newspaper stories and some television coverage had suggested I had, I felt as if I had lost my self-respect. I was afraid to call my manager, Sam Halvorsen, because I knew he would have been inundated with calls from my sponsors when the news broke back home in Australia as people usually believe what they read.

'Then I called my girlfriend Kellie and told her the real story and it was tough telling her. It was the same with Mum and Dad and even though I knew they would be understanding it didn't ease the pain. I thought of what my friends in Tasmania and all those young kids who look up to me might be thinking—that hit home the importance of making sure I do the right thing whenever I'm in the public eye.

'Back in India I felt as if everyone I walked past was glaring at me. I was so upset with myself for allowing the situation to arise and with all the bad press that followed, I wished the ground would open up and swallow me.

'I didn't know for sure how my team-mates felt about it deep down because I know it would have put pressure on them as well. And I had no idea what the captain or the selectors thought. Some crazy things run through your mind in situations like that.

'Ian Healy was a big help. He took me aside and we had a long discussion about how to handle the situation, in fact most of the guys were really supportive. In the end the players stirred me up about it and made jokes, and that was probably the best thing for me. They wanted me to try and laugh about it and get it out of the way so that we could all concentrate on the job at hand, but the hurt stayed with me for some time.

'What was written in the very first newspaper article was absolute rubbish and I can sympathise with how some other people have been treated by the British tabloids. It was simply gutter journalism and it had the potential to ruin my career over a nothing incident that was blown out of all proportion.'

The incident left its mark on Ricky and a realisation that he had more of a responsibility being an Australian cricketer than he thought.

'I learned a lot from that time and realised that there is more to representing Australia than just playing the game. I used to go about my business considering myself first and cricketer second, but now I have to ensure the priorities are the other way around.

'It was a bugger of a way to be made to realise that I am a Test cricketer with a fairly high profile. And that I have a responsibility when I'm in public.

'It can be tough because I have always been a bloke who likes to go down to the pub with the boys and have a good time, but it is just a matter of adapting. I still go into town at home in Launceston and have a few beers, but now it is only a few beers. I don't overdo it as I have done sometimes in the past. It was a horrible experience but one which I will make sure never happens again.'

But Ricky again hit the headlines, this time in Sharjah at the end of the Coca-Cola Cup series against India in April, 1998.

Ricky had been at the crease for about 45 minutes and he and Mark Waugh were well on the way to building a match-winning partnership. The pair had broken the back of the Indian attack taking more than 80 runs off 12 overs.

Harbhajan Singh was brought into the attack to quell the run-rate but Ricky had other ideas and took to the spinner in his second over, belting him for four and the next ball he lofted over mid-wicket for six.

Ricky danced down the wicket to the spinner's subsequent ball but missed, and Ricky was caught short of his crease as wicket-keeper Monglia whipped the bails off for a successful stumping.

Harbhajan Singh raced down the wicket towards Ricky and uttered expletives as the two players stood face to face. It was a crucial wicket for the Indians and Harbhajan was intent on expressing his feelings.

Ricky was also pumped with emotion. He knew he had played a poor shot and his dismissal put the Indians back in the game.

Having Harbhajan less than an arm's length from his face fuelled the situation and Ricky responded to the bowler's verbal abuse and unsportsmanlike antics.

'The Sharjah incident was probably the result of me being over-competitive but it had the potential to get quite nasty,' he says. 'I had just hit seventeen-year-old Indian spinner Harbhajan Singh for six and the next ball he slipped past me, and I was out stumped.

'I was really disappointed with the shot I played and when I looked up Harbhajan was right in my face giving me the finger and really mouthing off.

'Had he been a few more metres away from me I would not have reacted like I did or at the most I would have given him a bit of lip as I walked past. I just over-reacted to the provocation. Some of the media guys labelled me a hothead and one even described me as a gifted but erratic young gun of Australian cricket.

'It was just one of those things and even though I copped a fine and I admit it was the wrong thing to do, I will always play the game as hard as I can. I'm not the sort of person who steps back from a confrontation but I did overstep the mark on that occasion. I did not instigate the confrontation but with hindsight I realise I should have handled the situation better.'

In the end it cost both players a $500 fine but Harbhajan Singh also copped a one-match suspension.

Ricky has also made the headlines with his successes.

While he has not cared too much about breaking records, he admits that breaking Dean Jones' record of 145 as the highest for Australia in a one-day international would have been worth doing.

Jones blasted his 145 for Australia against England at the 'Gabba in Brisbane during the 1990–91 season. And Ricky matched Jones' record in a match against Zimbabwe at Delhi in a round of the Pepsi Cup in April, 1998.

'Had I known that the record was within my grasp before I decided to hit out I might have got it,' he says. 'I had no idea about the record until I came back into the change rooms and Steve Waugh nudged me and said I should have tried to break Deano's record. It didn't make too much difference to me at the time but on reflection it would have been great to have my name on that sort of record.

'A lot of the Australian players say I bat a lot like Deano and while I have never taken that much notice or tried to copy anyone in particular there must be some resemblance because a few players have mentioned it to me, including Shane Warne and he should know because he played hundreds of games with Jones for Victoria both in Tests and one-dayers.

'But I was very pleased with the innings, especially finding the middle early on. My first half-dozen or so scoring shots were boundaries but once we had the field back a bit we just built the total on ones and twos.'

Ricky scored the runs off only 157 balls and included 18 fours and a six. He also shared a near-record partnership with one of his best mates Mark Waugh. The pair put on a stand of 219 which unfortunately fell only five runs short of Allan Border and Dean Jones' all-wicket record stand they put on against Sri Lanka at the Adelaide Oval in 1984–85.

'I probably haven't enjoyed myself as much in a one-day international as I did that day. Batting with Junior [Waugh] was a buzz because we are pretty good mates and surprisingly we had not shared a lot of big partnerships since I made it into the Australian team.'

The rivalry becomes intense

'The Sharjah incident is an indication of how fiercely competitive the game is these days and while it has always been played with great passion at international level the after-match get-togethers which were once as much a part of cricket as the game itself have disappeared.

'At the start of each international series, whether it be one-day or Test, Tubby makes the effort to have a few drinks with the opposition players after each day's play but usually it ends up with each team going their own way. I think that the rivalry is so intense these days that the camaraderie that once existed between all nations has been lost from the game.

'We got on well with the South Africans during their most recent tour and that was the best it's been since I've been playing at Test level, but even then we only had the odd drink or two during the series. It would be great if Test cricketers could mix and get on like the old days. I don't see anything wrong with players from opposing nations getting together socially after matches. After all we all have a common interest and having a friendly relationship off the field shouldn't change the competitiveness once we get out in the middle.

'For example, the competition between AFL footballers on the field is as fierce as it gets, but most of the top players from various sides mix socially and many of them work together in the media. I hope that one day that special off-field camaraderie that existed once returns to the game.'

Chapter twelve

A PROFESSIONAL GAME

WHEN Ricky was still making his way in Shield cricket there was much speculation about his future at international level. Most of the top sportspeople in Australia and overseas had opted to secure personal managers to look after their business affairs and prominent Sydney-born and Hobart-based businessman Sam Halvorsen approached Ricky with the view to help him secure some sponsorship deals.

'Sam called me and suggested we have a talk about him managing me,' Ricky says. 'I told him I was still only a grade cricketer for Mowbray and that it might be a bit soon to have a manager. However he convinced me it could do no harm so we struck a deal.

'He made a lot of sense. The demands on Test cricketers are far greater than people imagine. It is great to have someone reliable who can take care of public appearances and sponsorship deals so I can concentrate on playing cricket.'

Sam Halvorsen has built a reputation as one of the most successful corporate property advisers in Australia but it was his love of sport which lured him into the field of professional player management. It was the combination of cricket and his connections in the corporate world that had him well placed to move into that career.

As Sam says: 'I had been thinking about becoming involved in player management for some time but it was in October 1994 when I was talking to Tasmania's cricket coach Greg Shipperd, who was singing the praises of Ricky, when I decided to make the move. He described Ricky as a prodigious talent who was coming through the ranks so I took Shippy's advice and called Ricky.

'We made contact and Ricky agreed to take me on board and since then we have built up a great working relationship.

'High profile sportsmen and sportswomen have much more pressure applied to them these days from the media and the corporate sector—the role of a manager is to ensure the athlete gains as many advantages from their talent as possible.

'I see my role in Ricky's career as one of a friend and confidant, and an older "head" trying to guide his off-field interests in a direction which will give him the greatest returns in the long term. Player management is about building relationships between the player and sponsors so that both parties are similarly advantaged from any dealings.

'Ricky is very marketable because not only is he an incredible talent, he has a friendly manner and is unaffected by his incredible rise to star status.

'Ricky has achieved so much for someone so young but his career has only just started and it is important that he has someone who can get him set up well financially and to be well placed with job opportunities at the end of his playing career. He is constantly in demand to endorse products, speak at functions and avail himself to the media. So with the exception of the very straightforward and spontaneous media interviews, Ricky is now armed with my business card. When approached about speaking engagements or endorsements, he simply says thank you, here's my manager's card. I can then sort out the wheat from the chaff and, more importantly, shield him from unnecessary over-exposure,' Sam says. 'Part of my role is to ensure he gets as much non-business leisure time as possible. With his cricket commitments being so intense it is important that when he does get a break there is as much free time as possible. When he has a week off I coordinate his commitments so that he has a lot crammed into two or three days but he has the rest of the week free. Spending time with his partner Kellie and his friends is extremely important to Ricky and part of my role is to arrange his business commitments so that there is some normalcy in his life. Unless you travel as much as a professional cricketer there is very little understanding of how much value players put on their spare time.

'But my most important role is identifying and negotiating deals with potential sponsors. Ricky already has a solid working relationship with Kookaburra, Oakley, the Tasmanian TAB, Tasmaid Pura [milk] which is part of the National Food Corporation and he will soon be linked with Hyundai. He is very conscious of his commitments to sponsors and he has a natural understanding of their importance in the short as well as the long term.'

* * *

Cricket as a career

Before the advent of World Series cricket, Australian Test cricketers had limited opportunities to carve lucrative careers from the sport compared to the players of the '90s. Today a Test cricketer can earn six-figure amounts annually from the game alone and as much again from endorsements.

'The players of the 1960s and '70s were usually employed by companies who used them for corporate functions or in other areas, and put them on modest retainers to enable them to spend time out of the country to play Test cricket,' Ricky says. 'The companies saw it as an advantage to have an Australian Test cricketer working for them. Today cricket is so demanding with players away from home for up to nine months of the year, it is no longer viable for companies to employ cricketers on that basis. But the cricketers of the '60s and '70s had a much tougher time trying to make a half-decent living out of the game.

'A regular Test and one-day player on contract is reasonably well-off and depending on his status in the team, he can make a tremendous living from the game. I have been able to buy a house and get myself set up for later in life and my career, hopefully, is only just starting.'

However, Ricky is aware of how demanding it is on a player striving to make it into an Australian team and make that sort of money. Playing Shield cricket and Mercantile Mutual one-day games are the only avenues to national selection.

'It is very hard financially on many Shield cricketers because many of them can't take on a career outside of the game because of the time State teams spend away from home playing either Shield cricket or one-day games. The sport is becoming so professional. Playing just Shield games earns a player about $27,000 a year but he is unable to take on any other full-time job because being a part of a Shield squad is so demanding. You are required to attend training every afternoon at 4p.m. on the dot and if you don't turn up they will simply choose someone else. Making the sacrifice was an easy decision for me because playing cricket is all I have ever wanted to do. I was single, young, had no financial commitments and I was still living at home so it wasn't a problem for me. But there are plenty of players with what it takes to make it to the top but for all the reasons I have mentioned, many probably will never achieve their goal.'

Facing the balls

When Ricky first played Shield cricket there was a sharp contrast between facing up to the best bowlers in the local grade competition and taking on the quality quicks and spinners at Shield level.

'When I first started playing first-class cricket for Tasmania I regarded Victorian Tony Dodemaide, NSW spinner Greg Matthews and Queenslander Carl Rackemann as the toughest to face. Dodemaide had just finished playing Test cricket and bowled with a little bit of pace, good outswingers and bowled very, very dry, sending down few loose deliveries.

'Rackemann was one of the best quicks I faced early in my career because he could get a ball to cut back into your ribs off a fairly good length and he was very hard to keep out. If you couldn't play a hook or pull shot against Rackemann you were in a bit of trouble.

'Greg Matthews was a class spinner and still taking heaps of wickets at international level when I first started in Shield cricket but in those days one of my weaknesses was handling spin—that is what I concentrated on most when I had my second stint at the Cricket Academy. When playing spin I was a bit too predictable because I stayed in my crease a lot. I had to work on my technique of getting down the wicket to the pitch of the ball to make a spinner change his length.'

West Australian Bruce Reid, who had his Test career cut short because of a chronic back injury, was regarded by most batsmen as one of the best left-arm quicks in the world and in his prime equal to Pakistan's Wasim Akram.

As Ricky says: 'Reid was another quick who made life tough and being a left-arm bowler made him even more lethal because he could get the ball to swing back sharply to the right-handers. When he really bent his back there were few quicker.'

The best bowlers at international level

West Indies
On the international scene Ricky regards West Indian Curtly Ambrose as the most feared combatant of the quicks.

'Curtly Ambrose is really quick and he is as good as anyone I've faced. I've only played against him twice but in the game against the Windies in Brisbane [1996] when there was a little bit in the wicket he bowled real quick, swung the ball both ways and he was very difficult to get away. He is the guy against whom you have to take risks to score runs. I think most of the guys in the Australian team would say the same thing. Curtly is so tall that when he lets the ball go it seems like he is only five metres away from you and when he knows there is something in the wicket for him he can get the ball to do amazing things.

'Courtney Walsh had a reputation for being as dangerous as Ambrose but when I faced him he seemed timid compared to the might of Curtly.'

England

'Andy Caddick was as good as any of the Pommie fast bowlers I have faced. He is deceptively quick and varies his pace well and can get a bit of movement both ways.

'Darren Gough is not all that quick but he is at you all the time and has the ability to come up with a scorcher every so often.

'Phil Tuffnell has copped some flack over the years but his performance against us last time we met was awesome. He got me out in both innings in that Test and my teammates who had played against him a lot over the years said it was the best they had ever seen him bowl.'

South Africa

'Sean Pollock is one of the best fast bowlers I've faced and his performance in Australia in the 1997–98 season was testament to his ability. Most batsmen regard Allan Donald as the most feared in the South African line-up but what Pollock did, in Adelaide particularly, was amazing. I played against him in South Africa when I went there with the Australian youth squad in 1992 and he was a bit special then. He is the son of former Test great Peter Pollock. He is sure to be around for a long time and is yet to reach his peak.'

Zimbabwe

'Heath Streak is easily Zimbabwe's best bowler I've faced.

He swings the ball both ways with his outswinger the most deadly and he can be extremely fast.'

Pakistan

'I have limited experience against Pakistan but Wasim Akram and Waqar Younis are both exceptionally fast bowlers. Wasim's record speaks for itself. In one-day games he is very hard to get away without taking risks.

'I didn't get to face Waqar when he was at his best but when he really bends his back, he can send them down as quick as Ambrose and he can get the odd one to lift sharply off a good length.'

Chapter thirteen

GIVING SOMETHING BACK

'THE development programs in place these days for kids are great compared to what was available when I was a kid at school,' Ricky says. 'When I was aged between ten and twelve there was nothing like the Kanga Cricket program and Milo development squads, and the special coaching clinics in schools taken mostly by Shield players.

'But now I do some of the coaching for the various programs in Tasmania and I love working with kids. I don't know whether I could coach kids every day but when I do get the chance to take the clinics it is a buzz. I partly enjoy working with the kids because it is something that I missed out on when I was their age. And it is amazing the amount of natural talent I see when I take charge of a Milo program—identifying the above-average players is never hard.

'The junior development programs in place today are essential because other sports like Aussie Rules still lure a lot of young kids away from cricket. The AFL has a very slick national program in place and I know that in Tassie a lot of kids who excel at both cricket and football end up choosing football because Tasmania has a national under-18 team, The Mariners. From there kids can find themselves in the annual draft and end up playing AFL footy.

'Cricket has to keep improving its junior development programs to stay a step ahead of the rest. The AIS Cricket Academy is fantastic and has helped make Australia the number one cricketing nation again. But there needs to be even more opportunities for young children to be introduced to the game and have the ones with well above average talent identified and groomed for first-class cricket.'

Port Arthur massacre: Tasmania's tragic day

Ricky is a community-minded individual who knows when to help out. On April 28, 1996 a crazed gunman, Martin Bryant, gunned down thirty-five people comprising men, women and children, at the historical site of Port Arthur on the Tasman Peninsula and the massacre sent shockwaves around the world.

When Ricky heard the news, like most Tasmanians, he struggled to come to terms with the tragedy; especially in a State which was renowned for its peace and tranquillity and one that liked to joke about being a half-century behind the times.

'It is still difficult to describe how I felt when I heard the news of the massacre and in the two months that followed there was a kind of cloud hanging over the State,' Ricky says. 'Every time I turned on the radio and television or picked up a newspaper it was there—a constant reminder of how a peaceful little town was turned into a graveyard.'

The survivors and the residents of the town were most

affected and when one of the Tasmanian Cricket Association executives, Tony Judd, suggested he and Ricky travel to Port Arthur to run some cricket clinics Ricky jumped at the chance.

'Juddy and I just wanted to help in any way we could and those kids really needed something to take their minds off what had happened,' he says. 'We spent a day visiting the schools in the area and setting up mini clinics, putting the kids through basic cricket drills, and we got an old footy and had a kick around the park. They seemed to enjoy it.

'The massacre hit all of us pretty hard but it didn't really hit me full-on until I got to the schools where there were flowers lying all over the place. You could see these kids were going through a very tough time in those first couple of weeks after the event.

'We went down to Port Arthur where it all happened—it was a very eerie experience. There were only a couple of people in the bar area when we arrived at the hotel for lunch but neither of us felt much like eating. It was like nothing I had ever experienced before and hopefully never have to experience again.

'I just felt empty and helpless. It was difficult to comprehend what it would have been like for those people at the site when that madman started shooting. I felt for the people who lost their lives and for the family members and close friends who had to deal with their tragic losses,' Ricky says. 'I reflected on how I felt when I had been dropped from the Australian team, but the anguish I felt then paled into insignificance compared to what the people of Port Arthur and the families of those killed had just been through.'

Chapter fourteen

THE TRIALS AND TRIBULATIONS ON TOUR

THE Australian cricketers have built a reputation for being great practical jokers when on tour and it didn't take Ricky long to fit into the mould.

In 1995 he was keyed up during a press conference held at Sydney's Mascot Airport just prior to the team boarding the Jumbo bound for the West Indies. It was Ricky's first tour with the senior Australian squad and Steve Waugh and skipper Mark Taylor had warned Ricky that he shouldn't be surprised if he became the brunt of a few practical jokes during the long flight to the Caribbean. The press conference passed in a flash and Ricky pondered what his team-mates might have in store for him. He decided he should strike the first blow.

'We were in business class and I found myself seated next to Tugga (Steve Waugh) who had the window seat and I was on the aisle,' Ricky says. 'We were all issued with a bag of goodies which included soap, toothpaste, shaving cream and breath freshener. Michael Slater was sitting opposite me and suggested I try the delicious breath freshener. So I cautiously flipped the cap off the bottle that I plucked from my goodies bag and timidly pressed the spray button—the breath freshener and shaving cream were in identical containers so I made sure I had the right one to spray in my gob. To my surprise it tasted as good as Slats said it did. I turned to Tugga to suggest he try some, but he was oblivious to what was going on around him. He had just lifted from his travel bag a brand spanking new laptop computer he had been given by IBM in which he was to document his West Indies Tour Diary. I nudged him and again suggested he try the breath freshener. But instead of the breath freshener I handed him the shaving cream. When his mouth filled with foam Tugga spat it out and it went all over the keyboard of his beautiful new laptop.

'He copped it sweet but he reminded me he had a memory like an elephant!'

Ricky learned the art of the practical joke quickly but by far the best prank he has conjured up was during a Test against South Africa in Adelaide. The Australians were in the field and Matthew Elliott had had to take time out because he had developed a blister on his foot, courtesy of a new pair of spiked shoes.

As Ricky remembers: 'When Herb [Elliott] returned to the field he had replaced his boots with sandshoes which were off-white and sporting an array of coloured stripes. He looked a bit funny so I walked over to umpire Steve Randell and suggested he use his walkie-talkie to contact the match referee and dummy up a false report card on Herb for wearing incorrect attire.

'When we finished the day's play, Randell came into the rooms and handed Tubby the fake report card which he then handed to Herb. The report said that Herb had violated the dress code and that he would be fined twenty-five per cent of his match payment.

'When Herb read the report he started to rant and rave while all the players who were in on the joke buried their heads in their lockers so he wouldn't see them roaring with laughter.

'The general consensus was to let Herb stew on it overnight but Tubby decided that wasn't in the best interests of team morale. Herb was relieved of his anguish when he came out of the shower.'

As Ricky pointed out, the joke was a payback for the time Elliott caught Ricky unawares during the Test against the West Indies at the 'Gabba in 1995.

'We had come off the field for lunch and I had taken my shoes off. When I put them back on my feet felt really wet, but I just thought I had trodden on something wet in the change rooms,' Ricky says. 'I got halfway out of the rooms and there was this squelching sound in my shoe. When I pulled it off there was this bloody great blob of ice-cream in the toe. I had a go at Herb over it but I copped flak from the other guys who said I could dish it out but couldn't take it!'

Boonie away from home

David Boon reached great heights during his thirteen-year Test career but he also earned a reputation for being a prankster and a truly great party animal who could be over-zealous when it came to consuming beer.

Ricky developed a great friendship with Boon especially during the Australian tour of the Caribbean in 1995. He has happy memories of some of the antics which went on particularly during the week after the tour ended.

'We went to Bermuda for some well-earned rest and recreation, and needless to say it was party mode most of the time,' he remembers. 'We had booked into this plush hotel and of course Boonie was the first to check out the bar facilities, which were very much to his liking.

'After testing a couple of glasses of their amber fluid, Boonie, Tubby, team physio Erroll Allcott and myself decided to do some exploring, and our only mode of transport was the moped. So we all grabbed one of these little motorbikes and set about checking out the scenery.

'But Boonie must have had some trouble with his moped because he fell way behind. We were a little worried so after a while we thought we had better head back and look for him. There was no sign of him so we decided he must have headed back to the bar and so we all set course for our hotel.

'We walked into the bar but Boonie was not in sight. We were a bit concerned. Then all of a sudden Boonie came strolling in with blood pouring from cuts on his legs, arms and face, and an unlit cigarette hanging out of the corner of his mouth. He had tried to do a U-turn at full speed and parted company with his moped sending him sliding along the road taking skin off most parts of his body, but especially his knees, arms and forehead.

'But before anyone could say a word Boonie just looked at us and said—"Has anyone got a light?".'

Dangerous fun
Ricky also had a run-in with the dreaded moped, assumed to be one of the safest modes of transport in Bermuda.

'The night after Boonie took his tumble, we all boarded our mopeds to do some sightseeing. About a kilometre from the hotel Heals [Ian Healy] stalled his bike and had trouble starting it,' he says. 'I fancied myself as a bit of a mechanical whiz so I offered him my bike and set about getting his started.

'It didn't take long to have the motor purring but on the way back to the motel I took a bend and the bike stalled, and somehow the back end wedged in guttering at the side of the road. When I planted the throttle, the rear wheel suddenly released and the bike and I flew straight into a pole. The bike was a complete write-off but luckily I came through unscathed.'

Belly bugs in India

There are always plenty of good yarns to tell after a tour of the subcontinent and one which Ricky remembers vividly involved former Test opener Michael Slater.

'The first few days of our trip to India for the World Cup in 1996 had most of the players wishing they had never been selected because everyone except Michael Slater was crook from the food. We were convinced Slats had a cast-iron stomach but about a week after we had recovered, Slats was hit by the bug.

'He was confined to his room, for obvious reasons, and on his third visit to the loo he discovered he was out of toilet paper. Slats rang reception and explained, in detail, to the guy on the other end of the phone. He requested a porter bring to his room two rolls of toilet paper and pronto. After fifteen minutes there was no sign of the porter, or more importantly the Indian version of Sorbent,

Punter—First Tests of a Champion

and Slats started to get agitated. He was just about to pick up the phone to give them a serve, when there was a knock at the door. He thought—at last! But when he opened the door there was this guy standing there with a tray. On it were two bottles of drink and he said to Slats—"Here's the two bottles of mineral water you ordered, sir".'

Chapter fifteen

THE TECHNIQUES OF A CHAMPION

ONE of the secrets of making it to the top in any sport is an athlete's ability to successfully work on weaknesses while at the same time finetuning strengths.

When Ricky was making his way through the ranks he was always more comfortable facing the quicker delivery than he was against spin. When he was inducted into the Cricket Academy, this was immediately identified and he spent hours each week working on the deficiency.

'I had no trouble in reading the spinners, it was my footwork that gave me most problems,' he says. 'I looked at some videos of myself and I couldn't really pinpoint the main problem. Eventually I discovered that if I changed my stance slightly I could get my feet in position quicker and that made all the difference.

'A lot of players place a big emphasis on performing well in the nets but that's not the case with me,' he says. 'If I have a bad net I don't let it get me down but for others, it can upset them for the entire day.

'David Boon told me that having a routine for net practice is very important and I have pretty much followed his lead.

'When I get into the nets I treat the early deliveries as if I am out in the middle in a match. I leave the wide deliveries to gauge the pace of the wicket and treat the good balls with respect.

'If I don't perform well in the nets I get someone to give me some throw-down practice. Someone throws the ball at me at a decent speed from about four metres away—that makes me move my feet into position quickly. If the ball is coming at you very fast from a short distance it makes you move your feet quicker plus you pay more attention to the flight of the ball. Sometimes I find a throw-down drill more useful than a fifteen-minute session in the nets—it really sharpens me up.'

Ricky has never tried to change his technique. Even during his time at the AIS there was never any pressure on him to change. As Ricky remembers: 'Rod Marsh told us at the Cricket Academy that he wasn't going to try and change our technique but instead try and perfect what we already had. Obviously to get to the Academy you have to have a fair bit of natural talent anyway, so he didn't want to take away anyone's flair. I spent a bit of time looking at videos of myself and in particular my footwork and how I play some shots. But at the end of the day it all boiled down to me making full use of what I've got and working hard on perfecting my natural technique.

'Watching videos of myself batting is a weird experience because it looks different on film than what it actually feels like at the crease. But one thing about videos is that they tell the truth. If you study them closely enough they can expose flaws in technique and once identified the player can set about correcting the problem. The most difficult thing to do is accept that you have a problem—once you get over that hurdle the corrective process starts. At the Cricket Academy we used to have two sessions a week watching videos of ourselves during batting practice. There are still times when I will watch a video of one of my more recent innings and then watch one of the old AIS videos and compare how I am playing shots now to then, and sometimes the difference is quite amazing. Although it is important to keep everything in perspective because it would be silly to race to the video cabinet every time you fail in an innings.

'There have been times that the videos have come in handy but they weren't a big help when I was out of form. There were days when I went to the crease determined to make it all happen but I knew from the outset that it was going to be a real struggle. I would be facing up and thinking that my hands didn't feel right, my feet were too far apart or the grip on the bat felt funny. Little things like that are very hard to combat when you are struggling to find the middle of the bat. Little things creep into my mind that I shouldn't even be thinking about—it makes it more difficult to regain form but I had to persevere. It sometimes takes only one good shot for it all to come together.

'It doesn't matter at what level you are playing—whether junior competition or Test level—the problems are the same, only the stakes are higher at Test level.

'Cricket is really a simple game but it is very easy to make it complicated and more often than not that gets a player into trouble. I have learnt that the more simple you make it for yourself the better chance you have to make runs.'

* * *

Ricky's favourite shots

'The pull shot is definitely one of my favourites and has been for as long as I can remember. I've scored a lot of runs from the shot although it also has led to my downfall. But maybe that's because I had chosen the wrong ball.

'Opposition bowlers work hard on bowling to a batsman's weaknesses—you are aware of that before you get to the crease. I have tried to develop a technique that gives me at least a couple of options for certain types of deliveries.

'I don't play a cut shot—that was one of my weaknesses I tried hard to rectify. In the end I came up with a shot that is more of a half-cut, half-drive.

'My technique stops me from playing the true cut. When I tried to cut, it always seemed that I was too close to the ball—it has something to do with my hands. It worried me for a while but when I started playing Shield cricket I found that I was not the only player at that level who didn't have every shot in the book. Mark Waugh can't play a textbook pull shot which is amazing considering he is such a magnificent strokemaker but he compensates for that with his other strokes. The cut is a high-risk shot and even though it would be good to have it in my kit, I still score a lot of runs with my adaptation of the shot.

'I love the hook shot—that is another shot I spend a bit of time on in the nets. And I score a lot of runs from straight drives. At one stage I developed a habit of square-edging deliveries back to the bowler but I just needed a slight adjustment in my wrist movement to overcome the problem. Like any sport, confidence plays a major role in coming to terms with flaws in your game. I found that the more I worried about a particular shot that was giving me trouble, the worse it became.

'It is a matter of getting solid practice in the nets and using the many aids available these days such as videos, which can help a batsman overcome a problem quickly.'

Fielding

'Ever since I can remember I have always spent time at practice sessions doing fielding drills,' Ricky says. 'For me, fielding is as important as making a century—a piece of brilliance in the field to instigate a run out can change the course of a game.

'Most players today have to be adept at fielding in many positions, although fast bowlers are primarily used as outfielders. I have worked very hard on my fielding and catching over the years and I'm sure that my ability in the field could one day save me from losing my place in a team if my batting isn't what it should be. But I get as much enjoyment out of fielding well as I do making runs.

'I usually field in the covers or square of the wicket but one day I might even be used as a reserve wicket-keeper. I kept wickets during my junior days and it was a position that came naturally to me. It would be tremendous if I could take on that role one day at first-class level. There was some suggestion that I might be handed the gloves at some stage in the one-day games if anything happens to Adam Gilchrist. I regard him as a great keeper and the natural to take over from Ian Healy.

'Healy is one of the best keepers I've seen—his departure from the one-day games to make way for Adam came as a bit of a shock. But I guess the selectors are trying to create opportunities and at the same time develop specialised one-day and Test teams. Thankfully I have been considered for both line-ups and I hope it stays that way for quite a while.'

Chapter sixteen

THE HIGHLIGHTS AND PITFALLS OF PROFESSIONAL CRICKET

In terms of his Test career, Ricky is only at the embryonic stage with his best years ahead of him. At the end of the 1997–98 season he had played in only eighteen Tests for a total of 1043 runs from 29 innings—his average only 37.25. This is well below his first-class career average which sits at 53.56 from 82 matches.

Ricky's 211 for Tasmania against Western Australia in a Shield game in November 1994 lifted his batting average to over 50 for the first time in his first-class career. While Ricky regards that knock as one of his best, the debut Test century for Australia against England at Headingly in 1997 was the most timely and exciting.

Ricky explains: 'It was my first game back in the Test team after bring dropped and there was an enormous amount of pressure on me to perform well. It was self-imposed pressure and that's the toughest to deal with but I was very determined to make the most of my chance and regain a regular place in the Test team.'

Australia had routed England courtesy of a magnificent

effort from quick Jason Gillespie who bagged seven wickets. The Poms had crumbled and were all out for 172.

But Australia started disastrously losing opener Mark Taylor, Mark Waugh and Greg Blewett cheaply.

'We had lost early wickets and when I strolled to the crease we were 4 for 50 and in a bit of strife. I definitely had a few butterflies as I faced up to the first ball. But when I pulled the third ball I faced to the boundary, the pressure seemed to lift. From that moment on I was in the zone and I felt as if nothing would stop me from reaching a century.

'I can't remember hearing the crowd or any of the conversations I had with Matthew Elliott out in the middle but that's the way it is when you are batting well and on top of your game. Matthew was striking the ball well and we set about resurrecting the innings. At the close of play, which was early due to rain, I was 84 and I felt as though I had achieved what I set out to do. It was a pretty good feeling when I walked into the dressing room. That night I had a good sleep and all I could think of was making my first Test hundred.

'Within the first half-hour of play the next morning, I had done it. I just trickled one down the leg side and took off as fast as my legs would carry me. When I reached the other end I raised my arm to wave my bat. I felt a mixture of elation, relief and satisfaction because I went into the game with something to prove and I had made my point the best way possible.

'I have been involved in some good partnerships and played some good hands in Shield, one-day games and other Tests, but so far my century at Headingly is head and shoulders above any of my other good knocks.'

In 1994 Ricky scored 161 for Tasmania against South Australia at the Adelaide Oval. It is one of his best innings in Shield cricket.

'Tassie had to win against SA to make it into our first Shield final and there was so much at stake. When I went into bat I had to make a big score to play my part in securing a victory.

'I had had good form going into the game but when there is that extra bit of pressure on, like it was for Tassie, sometimes it can turn the tide against you. As it turned out we all handled the pressure well in that match and we won to take us into our first Shield final. So it was not only one of my highest scoring innings but one of the most satisfying from a team perspective.'

Under the Southern Cross

Australia's victory song after each win in a Test match or one-day series final is now as traditional as the famed 'baggy green cap'. Penned by Rod Marsh and sung with great pride in the privacy of the change rooms at the end of a Test match or one-day final, the exact words to *Under the Southern Cross* are known only to those who have had the privilege of playing in a winning Test or international limited-overs team for Australia.

Ricky first experienced the emotion of singing the song in Barbados after Australia had scored a ten-wicket win over the West Indies in the First Test of the 1995 tour of the Caribbean. As he remembers: 'Naturally I had heard a lot about the traditional song and when the boys launched into it after the Barbados Test win, with Boonie leading the chorus, the hairs on the back of my neck stood to attention.

'It was unbelievable how the song got to me—it was probably right at the moment when the boys were in full voice that I felt a sense of belonging and a real part of the team.

'After every Test win, the change rooms are cleared of everyone except the players and team officials and then we launch into the song. The words are sacred to everyone in the room.'

When David Boon retired from international cricket, Ian Healy was given the honour of leading the victory song and when he was dropped from the one-day line-up for the balance of the 1997–98 season in Australia, Ricky received the shock of his life—he was to lead the song!

'When Heals rang me and told me he wanted me to lead the victory song in the one-day series I was shocked. It came like a bolt out of the blue but I was rapt that Heals chose me to do it.

'When we won the World Series one-day final against South Africa in Sydney I couldn't believe how nervous I was before I had to jump up on a table and lead the boys in the song. My mouth was dry and I felt the old ticker start to speed up, but once I blurted out the first line I was all right.

'It was a bit easier after we won the one-day series in India and hopefully I'll have it down to a fine art by the end of next season.'

Hazards of touring

Few players ever escape the dreaded stomach bugs contracted during tours of the subcontinent and Ricky is no exception.

'Most players get crook on the Indian tours and the first

time I visited the country I was laid up for a couple of days from something I ate. The worst hit for me was on the way home from my second tour of India.

'It never hit me until I arrived home in Australia but I was in a lot of strife because I had to get off a plane and head straight to Hobart for a Shield game.

'For that whole game I must have been off the ground at least once every hour to empty my stomach out.

'Whatever bug I had contracted, it prevented me from keeping food down for any length of time. We would go out for dinner and I would be hungry, but I could only take a couple of mouthfuls and then I would be crouching over with stomach pains. That lasted for about six weeks. I lost so much weight and when you are already as skinny as I am, weighing in at about 75kg, it can really knock a bloke about.'

Ricky survived the stomach bug on Australia's most recent tour of India and Sharjah.

'I missed the stomach bug the last tour and that was a real bonus, but I still managed to get a touch of sunstroke coupled with a bad dose of dehydration.

'I batted one day and scored 155. I felt all right when I came off the ground but I guess when the adrenaline stopped pumping my whole body started aching and I knew I was in trouble. When I got back to my room and lay down I started shivering and had hot flushes, so I decided to take a hot bath but that was useless. My head started pounding, much worse than a bad headache and then came the vomiting. I had to keep pumping the fluids into me but no sooner would I down a glass of water than I'd be bringing it back up again.

'What really had me worried was my inability to focus.

Everything was blurry and the harder I tried to concentrate the stronger the pain got in my head.

'This happened two days prior to a Test match but the way I felt I could not have cared less about playing cricket. Luckily it passed in twenty-four hours and I have never had anything like it since and that's how I want it to stay.

'I think having to play in such hot and humid conditions is a joke,' Ricky says. 'The first one-day game we played in India it was 48 degrees Celsius and the humidity was running at about ninety-five per cent which is unbearable. You shouldn't have to play in those conditions. As soon as you walk onto the ground your shirt and pants are soaking.

'We fielded first that day and after 50 overs I was knackered and when I went into bat I only made 12. When I got back to the rooms I just collapsed in a heap.'

Of Ricky's three visits to the subcontinent the most recent tour was, in his opinion, the best.

As he says: 'The hotels we stayed at had decent restaurants with quality food with much more variety and were definitely more nutritious than in the past.

'My first trip to India was with the AIS Academy and we stayed in hotels quite a few rungs down from the top quality establishments. It was the bare essentials and nothing more.

'One thing that was very noticeable this most recent tour was the work that has been done to upgrade the conditions at the venues,' Ricky says. 'They have done a lot of work on improving the condition of the playing surfaces at most venues and the amenities such as change rooms also have been upgraded. Some of the grounds we played at only had barricades around holes in the ground which served as a toilet. Before we left our hotel each day we had to make sure the toilet paper was packed in with our cricket gear.

'The stench also can be off-putting and the smell we had to tolerate during the First Test in Madras this most recent trip was unbelievable. The ground sits next to a river. The water in the river is black and infested with insects and laden with water buffalo, and when there is no breeze the smell just wafts across the ground. It is the worst smell anyone could imagine.'

Ricky never ceases to be amazed at the number of people who inhabit the subcontinent.

'It is just amazing that over 965 million people are crammed into a country the size of Western Australia,' he says. 'Everywhere you go there are thousands of people and no open spaces. That's something that we Australians definitely take for granted.'

And being an Australian cricketer walking the streets of Calcutta can lead to a run-in with the law, as Ricky found on his first tour.

'A couple of the guys needed to replace some hand luggage that had been damaged so I joined them for a stroll down to the market. We had only been looking in the shops for about fifteen minutes when the police arrived. They grabbed us and told us to go straight back to our hotel because we were causing a public nuisance.

'When we looked behind us there were about 1000 people gathered in the street just gawking at us because they recognised us as Aussie cricketers.'

Ricky was appalled at the living conditions in some of the areas the team visited during the most recent tour.

'It is common to see people with no arms or legs in the streets begging for money and women carrying little babies who obviously have not had a decent feed in ages. There are also people living in the gutters. It was nothing to drive up a road and see hundreds of people in the gutters or hiding under primitive forms of shelter on the side of the road.

'It was very depressing but it made me realise how lucky we are here in Australia.'

Learning how to win

'Despite us winning the one-day series in India we went into the Coca-Cola Cup final in Sharjah as the underdogs. The team wanted to win the Sharjah final badly—that is the standard we set for ourselves, we want to win every game we play and definitely every final we contest.

'As you grow up with the sport the most important thing you learn when you first play cricket is to have fun. As you get older and the competition becomes more intense from grade competition to first-class level, the pressure grows and the difference between winning and losing has more meaning. When you are playing for Australia and at home there is an even greater expectation placed on the eleven blokes who line up in a game. Especially in a final because whatever the population is in Australia, all but a couple or a few bus loads of supporters want you to win.

'The Australian team plays at its best when we are all enjoying ourselves and that's hard to do when you are getting flogged every time you go out there. Winning gives you that edge and opportunity to have a bit of fun.

'The blokes playing for Australia at the moment are a very close-knit group and while we all enjoy everyone else's success, we also share their failures. We can go out there and tackle the game professionally but at the same time be out having fun—that's when you really know you're in the zone of success,' Ricky says.

Ricky made his debut for Australia at a time when the team was performing well and it has continued to do so to the end of the 1998 tour of the subcontinent.

'When I first started playing Shield cricket with Tassie we didn't win a lot of games and there is an enormous difference when you are playing for your country and enjoying the success we have had in the past couple of years.

'Other than being dropped after playing only three Tests, I probably won't reflect on Australia's performances from the late 1990s until I have finished playing Test cricket. And other than losing my place in the team, I haven't experienced a lot of lows because since I have played for Australia the team has won more games than it has lost.

'No matter what sport it is, you have to learn to handle defeat to fully appreciate winning. A positive attitude and a desire to win are two of the main atttributes needed to make it to the top in any sport.

'There is no doubt that confidence breeds success and that's why Boonie is such an asset as captain of the Tasmanian Shield team because he has played at international level for so many years and tasted the big victories. And he has the ability to instill that feeling in the State players.

'Winning is not everything but it sure beats the hell out of losing.'

Time away from home
Playing cricket at the highest level puts an enormous strain on players' personal relationships and there have been marriage break-ups and many long-standing relationships

aborted for the sake of the game. Ricky has been in a relationship with Kellie Sainty for almost five years and somehow the pair have managed to find a way to keep the fire burning between them without Ricky compromising his career.

'During the 1997–98 season I spent eight days at home in five months. That has to put a bit of pressure on a relationship but I am very lucky to have someone who really understands. Kellie and I have been together almost five years but I guess in that time we have probably only spent about two years together as a couple in real terms.

'I miss Kellie like crazy when I'm playing overseas because those trips are always a long haul but I'm sure it is a lot harder on the wives and girlfriends of the players,' Ricky says. 'When we are away we have always got things to do when we are not playing cricket and a unique mateship exists within the team because we pretty much all share the same feelings as far as our relationships are concerned.

'I know that Kellie is often left to sit at home just waiting for my phone call and that's why I am fastidious about calling when I say I will. She obviously has her own life to lead while I'm away because she plays sports and has a circle of friends, but she still spends a fair amount of time just sitting at home and I'm sure it is a similar situation with other players' girlfriends.'

When Ricky was selected to go to England in 1997 Kellie decided she would take time off work to join him on tour but she was left with a tough decision to make. Her employer would not agree to her taking the time off so she resigned.

Ricky says: 'It was a pretty big call for Kel to quit her job but I'm glad she made the trip. There is a lot to be said for having your partner close by when you are away on tour.

'It's funny that I have such a serious relationship because I had never been one to worry too much about girls. In my teens I preferred to go to the footy with my mates—girls came in second behind sport. But now Kellie is probably my best mate. I can talk to her about anything and she really understands what I'm about and I am there for her.'

A partner's point of view

'When Rick and I first started seeing each other seriously he was only playing Shield cricket and our time apart wasn't too taxing but since he moved to Test level there have been times when I thought the relationship would break down,' Kellie says. 'There is no denying life is difficult when Rick is away for any great length of time but I have learned to cope and I wouldn't change our relationship for the world.

'I have really good friends and family and without them I think it would be very difficult to cope. There were times when I would have to leave work and go home and break down and cry because I was missing him terribly, but thankfully I have tremendous friends who I could rely on to help me get through each little crisis.

'The telephone and faxes are marvellous inventions—the phone is my most cherished possession in the house when Rick is away,' she says. 'Rick calls me every day when he is away, whether he is in England or India and we have at least a few minutes catching up.

'It does get easier and having other interests such as sport is probably more important to me when Rick is away. I have also developed some good friendships with the partners of some of the other Australian players. I often get on the phone to them and that always cheers me up.

'I get on really well with Mark Waugh's partner Sue Porter since the first time we met when I travelled with Rick on a tour of New Zealand in 1995. Sue would ring me each day and get me out of my room—she showed me the ropes, so to speak. I learned really quickly that on tour the men are good at cricket and the girls are good at shopping. Sue was a brilliant teacher in the art of shopping till you drop!

'But travelling with Rick on tour is a rarity and while he is away I often think of special little things I can do to make his homecoming special. One time he arrived back home on February 15 so I had a special Valentine's Day present for him—a half-dozen heart-shaped helium balloons, a basket filled with an array of alcohol and chocolates, and other little things that I knew he would appreciate and that he wouldn't have had while on tour.

'Going out to dinner at a restaurant is nothing wonderful for Rick, it is something he does every other day, so we think of other fun things to do.'

Kellie had little interest in cricket until she met Ricky and now she is one of the game's most ardent fans. As she says: 'You can't help but take an interest when it is the man in your life's profession but I admit the game has me hooked and I get immense pleasure out of watching Rick play. I am also coming to terms with how to share the highs and lows.'

Kellie becomes Ricky's personal at-home secretary while he is away on tour and some of her tasks might seem a bit far-fetched to the uninitiated.

'One of the things I do for Rick when he is overseas is record some greyhound races and play them back to him over the phone and I cut out a whole heap of sports clippings from the newspapers and stick them to A4 sheets of paper and fax them to him, wherever he is at the time. It just makes him feel that much closer to home and I get so much enjoyment out of doing it, so it cuts both ways.

'I play netball and that keeps me fairly busy with training and playing, and it's terrific when Rick is home and he comes to watch me play. It's a role reversal and I know Rick enjoys it as much as I do.'

Whenever the subject of marriage is raised, Ricky and Kellie just look at each other and smile. Kellie says: 'We have talked about marriage but we both want to wait another couple of years to see where life takes us.'

The best of mates

One of the hidden bonuses of playing Test cricket for Australia is the forming of off-field friendships.

'All of the guys get on so well together off the field which is probably one of the reasons why Australia has had such a good side over the past four or five years,' Ricky says. 'We are good mates and after matches I go out for an evening meal with three or four different players each night of the week.

'Mark Waugh is probably my closest friend of the guys in the Australian team and there are times when we might just shoot off together one night to have a punt, but it would only ever be one night a week or a fortnight because it is very important to the team morale that we stay a close-knit unit and not have little groups developing.

'Tubby has always stressed that it is very important to team spirit that we all stay together as much as we can, especially when we are away on tour to places like India and Pakistan where the team has to be at its best to survive and do well. It only takes one guy to be a loner and not have the same goal as the rest of the team to upset the apple cart. The better we get on off the field the better chance we have of achieving on-field success.'

Ricky is the youngest player in the Australian team when Jason Gillespie is out of the line-up, which should come as no surprise considering he has been the baby of most teams he has played in since he was thirteen.

'When I first started playing Shield cricket I was made to feel like the baby of the team but that never happened when I made it into the Australian team,' he says. 'You see, everyone is treated as an equal in the team. That is another reason why we get on so well together. One of the best things about playing in this Australian team is that all the players are prepared to share in someone's disappointments and failures as well as their successes.

'In India after the last Test there, I recall sitting down with Greg Blewett who was worried about his loss of form and he was pondering his future. I spent some time talking him through it because I knew what he was going through. Ian Healy realised what was going on and he came over to talk to Blewey as well.

'All the players care about each other. It is a very special bond that exists. Even when I got dropped I had a couple of calls from a few of the boys, but I was at home in Tassie and went straight back into playing Shield where I relied a lot on State coach Greg Shipperd to help me through some tough patches.'

Chapter seventeen

FUN AND FRIVOLITY ON AND OFF THE FIELD

WHEN a player makes his way into the Australian team it is common practice for him to be branded with a nickname if he hasn't already established one.

Ricky loves to have a bet and his unrivalled passion for greyhound racing, which was well-known by the Australian squad, therefore Shane Warne quickly dubbed Ricky Ponting 'Punter'.

Ricky says: 'I am very comfortable with the nickname—it probably came in handy when my manager was negotiating a sponsorship deal with the Tasmanian TAB.'

Ricky had his first brush with the racing industry as a child. 'Dad trained and raced greyhounds and from the first time I went to a dog meeting in Launceston I was hooked. Dad used to have a bet and he would listen to the races on the radio, and I started to pick out numbers to have a bit of an interest. I liked horse racing but there was something special about greyhounds. I decided a long time ago that if ever I did well at cricket I would race a couple of greyhounds and I stuck to my word.

'It is a lot cheaper to race a greyhound and while the prize money isn't anywhere near as much as it is for thoroughbreds, your return for outlay is probably a lot better in the long run, provided they can win a few races of course.'

Ricky had success with the first dog he raced—Arundel Earl.

'Arundel Earl won two races for me but he broke down. Then I got very lucky with his replacement, Elected. I bought him as a racing dog and he ended up winning eighteen races, so with prize money and what I won on the punt, he was a good investment.

'Josie's Joy was my next dog and she won twelve races and is soon to drop a litter, and hopefully a couple of her pups will develop into good racers.

'My Self was the next to join the kennel and I paid $5000 for her which is a lot. But she has already won thirteen races and has the potential to be an excellent broodbitch.'

With so much success, like everyone who ventures into racing, Ricky was due for a lemon and it looks like his $5000 investment in a well-bred Victorian dog named Ruling Light may be the first to leave a bitter taste in his mouth.

As Ricky says: 'Ruling Light has been a disappointment but if he doesn't live up to expectations I will still be well in front on what I've invested so far.'

Ricky is a regular at the Launceston greyhound meetings at the White City track on Monday nights when he is not on tour and he is determined not to let his status as a Test cricketer interfere with his racing interests.

'I was fourteen when I went to my first dog meeting at White City and I make a point of going to as many meetings as I can when I am home having a break from cricket. I like betting on greyhounds because with only eight dogs in a race it reduces your chances of losing and if you follow the form closely enough it is a lot easier to back winners.'

Ricky also has taken a share in a racehorse with Mark Waugh, who also is a mad keen punter and lover of the racing game.

With such a keen interest in racing, Ricky was a natural to be selected by the Tasmanian TAB as its ambassador and high profile figurehead for most of its advertising campaigns.

'The TAB has been fantastic to me and when my manager, Sam Halvorsen, secured the deal, I was rapt. I wouldn't endorse anything I didn't believe in and while there might be some people out there who don't go much on having a punt, as far as I'm concerned there is no harm in it as long as it is done in moderation and according to what you earn.

'After all, racing and gambling are as much a part of being an Australian as eating a meat pie at the footy.'

Musselroe Bay

Finding things to fill in any spare time has never been a problem for Ricky. If he isn't honing his skills in the nets or out on the golf course, he is hard at it, studying the racing form and stationed at his local club watching the nags and the greyhounds on Sky Channel.

But one of his unpublicised recreational pastimes is fishing.

His passion for dropping a line goes back to his younger days at Musselroe Bay, Tasmania's far North-east Coast where his grandparents, Connie and Charlie Ponting, have a holiday shack.

'I love fishing. I can spend a whole day dangling a line and not care if I don't get a bite. It all started at Musselroe Bay when we used to stay at Nan and Pop's shack during the school holidays. Pop had a little boat with a small outboard that we used to take offshore and I don't think we ever came back without at least enough fish for a feed that night.

'There's something about dangling a line that's so relaxing and while I don't get a chance to do much fishing these days I have made plans to get up to the Great Lakes in the Central Highlands in Tassie for a spot of trout fishing next season.

'Dad and I used to do a bit of trout fishing and we would make a day of it, walking up and down the river, sometimes well into the night, in search of a big brown—sometimes we'd get lucky.'

Musselroe Bay also provided Ricky with his personal cricket camp come every school holidays.

'When we first went to Musselroe Bay we had a caravan and I used to spend most of my time at my relations' shack just around the corner from the caravan park.

'Sue and Darrel Filgate had a shack on a big block and it was well grassed and I reckon I spent ten hours a day at their place playing cricket with their sons Darren, who was killed a few years ago in a car accident, and Scott.

'I reckon I made more centuries at Musselroe Bay than I'll make in a lifetime of first-class cricket. My parents or grandparents used to wander up to the Filgates' shack to retrieve me for meals because I had no sense of time, especially if I was batting.

'Most days I would have a quick bite for breakfast and they wouldn't see me again until tea time.'

Collecting memorabilia

Watch any Test match or one-day international and at the end of the game, no matter what the result, players will make a charge for the stumps to secure a piece of memorabilia from the encounter.

Ricky hasn't learned to be quick enough off the mark but he has firm intentions of one day setting up a cricket room in his home full of cricket memorabilia from his playing days.

'I have a few specially printed sets of Test photographs signed by a heap of players that I brought back from the last tour of England but so far that's all I've really collected that isn't a personal memento.

'I keep one of my shirts and a bat from each series. They are safely tucked away in storage and they'll make their way into the cricket room someday.

'I've kept all the bats I used to get first-class centuries and I will get them done up one day and set up a nice display case at home, but there's plenty of time for that stuff. There are also some little keepsakes that I've stashed in a drawer at home that will probably mean a lot more in thirty years than they do today.

'A lot of the guys have a really good collection, especially Steve Waugh—he is unbelievable when it comes to cricket trivia. Tugga is a regular walking encyclopedia on the game and I reckon he will have one of the best showcases of memorabilia about when he leaves the game. His diaries have already been published and have been very popular.

'I will probably start keeping diaries on future tours. They should be great to reflect on when I've finished playing.'

Chapter eighteen

RICKY LOOKS TO THE FUTURE

'THE decision to field specialist one-day and Test teams last season is a step in the right direction but it did cause some tension within the ranks,' Ricky says. 'Having Tubby as Test captain and Steve [Waugh] skipper of the one-day team took a bit of getting used to, but all the players have accepted it now.'

When Mark Taylor met with the Australian Cricket Board soon after arriving back in Australia from the India tour, many of the players believed he would call it quits as captain.

'I think a few players, and I was one, thought Tubby would chuck it in after India, but as soon as he reapplied for the Test captaincy we knew nothing would change from what we had in India and here in Australia at the start of the year.

'There is no doubt the game calls for two types of player these days and there are definitely those who are one-day specialists and there are a few who sit better with Test cricket. Obviously the selectors believe Tubby is a much better Test player and is not at his best in one-day games, but it is a fairly fine line in his case.

'Tubby is a fighter and a battler and he has done bloody well for Australia over the years. It wouldn't surprise me to see him again captain the one-day team because cricket can be a funny game at times—he would only have to hit a purple patch to be back playing international one-dayers.'

Playing under two captains, so vastly different in their approach to the game, had the potential to disrupt the team spirit.

As Ricky says: 'The players handled the change well because it wasn't as if someone none of us knew was walking in to take over the one-day captaincy. We all have the utmost respect for Steve Waugh as a cricketer and as a mate, so the transition from one skipper to the other was relatively easy, even though they have very different approaches to the game.

'I rate Tubby the better captain because he is a better communicator and he is also probably a little bit quicker a thinker. But one-day cricket is a lot harder to captain than Test because you have to make frequent changes. In Test cricket the field can stay pretty much the same for long lengths of time.'

Taylor lost the one-day captaincy through a loss of form with the bat and because there was so much pressure from in-form players champing at the bit to secure a one-day spot. Selectors had no option in the end but to give Tubby the heave-ho. The big surprise omission from the one-day line-up was wicket-keeper Ian Healy.

'I think everyone was shocked when Healy was dumped from the one-day side because his record was pretty good.

There was a lot of pressure on to get Gilly [Adam Gilchrist] into the team and because he was a specialist left-hand batsman as well as a top keeper, he finally got the nod. But everyone felt for Heals. He is such a tremendous asset as a team player as well as being a brilliant keeper and so proficient with the bat. Heals has saved Australia with the bat in Tests and one-day games on numerous occasions—he hasn't lost any of his sparkle with either bat or gloves.'

The captaincy issue

'There has been a lot of speculation about me becoming captain of Australia but it shouldn't even be an issue at this stage of my career,' Ricky says. 'I know nothing can stop the media from coming up with those sort of rumours but as far as I am concerned the captaincy role for Australia is not something I want to think about at this point in time.

'Mark Taylor is a great captain and his international career almost came to an end when we returned home from Sharjah over the dual captaincy roles. The pressure of being a captain is enormous—I am still only twenty-three with plenty of time on my side.

'Steve Waugh is also doing a great job of captaining the one-day team and while he takes a different approach to games than Tubby, he has plenty to offer. And I know Shane Warne has put his hand up for the captaincy role should either Tubby or Steve step down or retire from the game.

'Warney plays the game hard and he already has been blooded as captain of Victoria. No doubt he too would be a good captain for Australia.

'When I was in Sharjah I was approached about captaining

the Australia-A side that went to the UK in July. I thought hard about it but I knew that I would be much better off taking a break from the game for a few months so I declined. That was good ultimately because another Tasmanian and a good mate, Michael DiVenuto, got the job.

'I am happy just to be a regular member of the team for the time being but I would be a fool not to want the greatest honour of all further down the track. And I am always thinking about the game like a captain when I'm playing. I try to anticipate bowling changes or changes in field placements, and sometimes I put my 10 cents worth in when I walk by the skipper.

'Cricket is a game of tactics and a captain must be able to read a game and have an ability to see flaws in a batsman's make-up and work with his bowlers to capitalise on those weaknesses. A captain also has to be a great on- and off-field leader and have the respect of all the players—that's probably one of the most important things about the job.

'I think I have what it takes to be a good captain and hopefully I will get the chance to prove it one day, whether it be for my home State, Tasmania, or for Australia.'

Advice for juniors

'When I was a kid I was told that you only ever get out of sport what you put into it—that would be my best advice to any youngster who had ambitions to play the game at the top level or had intentions of making cricket or any other sport a career. And there is a lot to be said for the adage—the harder you work, the luckier you get.

'A lot of kids also don't understand the difference between

hearing and listening. And good eye contact is what they should develop because that makes you concentrate more on what the other person is saying.

'When I was at the Academy, Marshy told us that everything needs to be stored in your brain as if it was a computer. Then sort through the stuff you need and axe the rest.

'Cricket these days can be a full-time profession although, like golf, only a select few make it to the top. But my motto is—if you have a dream, go for it and don't let anyone or anything stand in your way.'

Public speaking

Before Ricky made his Test debut in 1995 he could have counted his public speaking engagements on one hand.

Ricky was never groomed for public speaking roles. Apparently it was like getting blood out of a stone just to get him to make a speech whenever he made his annual visit to the podium to collect awards for his cricketing achievements.

But fame has its way of stirring the fire within and since his return from his first and successful Ashes tour of England in 1997, the shy kid from the sleepy hollow of Mowbray has come out of his shell.

'I was always scared of standing up in front of people to make speeches and the thought of having to spend more than five minutes in front of a microphone talking about myself used to send shivers up my spine.

'I never had any trouble sitting down with a group of kids at cricket clinics or at schools and talking to them. There are a certain number of speaking engagements in the offing as a result of me being a Test cricketer. I suggested to my manager that he only accept one or two each year.

'That idea went down like a lead balloon and so I agreed to work my way up to a half-dozen or so gradually. But I guess it is like anything else in life, the more you practise something the better you become.

'I found that talking to people about my experiences overseas, outside of cricket not only made me sound more interesting but it also helped me enjoy what I was doing. People were interested in how I perceived life on the other side of the world from first-hand experience and when you see how some people have to live in ghettos and in squalor on the subcontinent it makes you realise just how well off we are in this country.

'People also love to hear stories about the other players and some of the funny things that happen on tour. So I guess the more Test cricket I play the better I'll be as a guest speaker.'

Chapter nineteen

THE STATISTICS OF A CHAMPION

IN Ricky's first year of first-class cricket he kept the statisticians busy as he combined personal milestones with rewriting the record books. Becoming the youngest to play Shield cricket for his State was first cab off the rank, closely followed by the youngest to make a Shield century for Tasmania.

In his first season of Shield competition in 1992–93 he notched 782 runs from 18 innings with a highest score of 125 against NSW at the SCG which was one of three centuries. The other two centuries also claimed the young player a record by becoming the youngest Tasmanian to score a century in both innings of a Shield match with 107 in the first innings at Bellerive and an unbeaten 100 in the second innings.

He reached 50 four times that season and finished with an average of 46.

In the field he snapped up nine catches and rolled the arm over 52 times conceding 24 runs although he failed to take a wicket.

His second season brought even greater joy, finishing

with a total of 965 runs from 22 innings with a highest score of 161 against South Australia in Adelaide. This helped steer Tasmania into its first Sheffield Shield final.

That was one of three centuries he scored that season and he again reached 50 four times for a season average of 48.25 and a career average of 47.22.

He had slightly more work with the ball sending down 150 balls for 88 runs but picked up two wickets to give him an average of 44, with his best effort 1 for 7 against SA in its first innings in Hobart.

The 1994–95 season saw Ricky take his statistics to international level as a member of the Australian squad touring the West Indies and as a member of the Young Australians tour of England.

Before leaving Australia that season he notched 772 runs in Shield cricket from only 12 innings and registered his highest first-class score of 211 against Western Australia at Bellerive Oval. That innings also gave him a record as it was his fifth consecutive century for Tasmania against WA taking his total from five innings against that State between March 1993 and November 1994 to 624 at an average of 124.8.

Another century at Bellerive against NSW, followed up with a 62 at the same venue, took his career average to 52.42.

He only played in one first-class game in the West Indies at Georgetown where he scored 19 in the first innings and did not bat in the second.

He played in seven matches on the Young Australians tour of England collecting 460 runs at an average of 46, reaching 50 four times and a best score of 103 not out against Worcester.

However, his career average after the England tour stood at 49.97. He also sent down 10 overs on that tour conceding 36 runs but was wicketless.

The 1995–96 season was Ricky's best. He notched 480 runs for Tasmania at the start of the season in Shield and a three-day match against Sri Lanka at an average of 68.58.

He then launched into his Test career against Sri Lanka in WA scoring 96 on debut which boosted his career average to an all-time high of 53.85.

A well-made 71 in the first innings of the Second Test bumped his career average to 54.10 but failing to get beyond 20 in his four subsequent innings dropped his average to 51.57.

The tour to India the next season had little effect on his average with it falling only marginally to 51.13 after four innings on the subcontinent.

Ricky was dropped from the Australian team after only two Tests against the visiting West Indies in which he failed in three of his four innings. At the end of the Second Test his career average had slipped to 49.98 but was a mere 19 against the West Indies.

Back in Shield cricket Ricky found form mid-season with a 94 not out against Victoria at the MCG and he finished the season in a blaze of glory with three consecutive centuries, two against South Australia at Bellerive and a match-winning 159 against Queensland at the same venue which lifted his average back up to 53.25. He finished the season with a career average of 52.69 which earned him a recall to the Australian team for the Ashes tour of England.

He played four county games at the start of the tour for an average of 48.40 which included 126 not out and 28 not out against Glamorgan at Cardiff.

He then made his Test debut in England at Headingly and notched his maiden Test century of 127, which took his average to a career best of 54.36. Departing England with an average of 53.66, his average during the tour was a staggering 63.44 from 12 innings with his Test average 48.20.

Ricky scored back-to-back centuries on his return to Australia in Shield cricket with 121 in the second innings against SA in Adelaide and an unbeaten 129 in the first innings against WA at Bellerive. He was unbeaten on 14 in Tasmania's second innings.

At the end of the Australian summer of 1997–98, which comprised three Tests each against New Zealand and South Africa, Ricky's career average stood at a solid 54.62.

From his four innings against NZ he scored 119 with a top score of 73 not out for an average of 39.67 but he fared much better against the South Africans against whom he notched 248 Test runs at an average of 49.60 with his best effort 105 in the first innings at the MCG. Ricky ended the 1997–98 season with a trip to India for a three Test series in which he managed only 105 runs for a paltry average of 23 with his highest score 60 in the first innings of the Second Test.

However he finished the tour with 365 runs and a highest score of 155, leaving his career average at 53.56 and only marginally below where it sat prior to the subcontinent tour.

Ricky's career averages against individual opponents are interesting. Internationally, his best performances have been against Sri Lanka against whom his average is 48.25, only marginally behind England at 48.20.

From limited contests against New Zealand his average is 39.67 and against the West Indies his first-class average is 27.50.

But by far his worst results have been against India with his average 18.86, although his overall Test average from only 28 innings is 37.25.

However, at Shield level, where Ricky has spent most of his short first-class career, he has amassed 3860 runs from 40 matches and 73 innings.

His performances against Western Australia have been exceptional, scoring 917 runs from 14 innings at an average of 83.36, and against whom he compiled his highest score of 211. His average against SA is 69.36 from 16 innings with a high score of 161, and his average against Queensland is similar at 67.73 from only 13 innings.

Ricky's international limited-overs career average at the end of the 1997–98 season was 38.68 from 55 games and a strike rate 71.50.

What the future holds

'Hopefully I will still be playing Test cricket for Australia in ten years time and whether it will be batting at number six, four or three it won't matter, as long as I'm out there. If I can remain focused and I don't develop any injury problems I would expect to be still playing when I am thirty-three or thirty-four.

'Mark Waugh is thirty-three and he has no major injury problems and hopefully I can keep myself in good shape to ensure my longevity in the game.

'As for playing for Australia, that will depend on my

performance but I should be a better batsman as I get older. Most players don't hit their peak until their late 20s so I have that to look forward to.

'The demands on players these days are far greater than in the 1970s and early 80s—most of the Australian players spend all but two months a year touring or playing in Australia. Keeping physically and mentally fit is so important, and that's why today there are very few players carrying excess weight. Gone are the days when you can hide poor fieldsmen, especially at one-day level, which is probably why the Australian selectors are now opting for a specialist one-day team.

'I am fortunate at the moment being considered for both Test and one-day games, and that's how I hope it will stay for at least the next five years. Ever since I was a teenager all I have ever wanted to do was make a living from cricket and so far all of my goals have been reached.'

PONTING, Ricky Thomas

Born: December 19, 1974 Launceston (TAS) (Age: 23)
Bats: Right-hand batsman
Bowls: Right-arm medium bowler

First-class Career

Debut: 1992-93 Tasmania v South Australia, Adelaide

Season	Country	M	Inn	NO	Runs	HS	Os	50	100	Avrge	Ct	St	Balls	Mdns	Runs	Wkts	Avrge	5	10	Best
1992-93		11	18	1	782	125	-	4	3	46.00	9	-	52	2	24	-	-	-	-	-
1993-94		12	22	2	965	161	-	4	3	48.25	13	-	150	5	88	2	44.00	-	-	1/7
1994-95		7	12	-	772	211	-	3	3	64.33	1	-	54	-	42	-	-	-	-	-
1994-95	West Indies	1	1	-	19	19	-	-	-	19.00	1	-	-	-	-	-	-	-	-	-
1995	England	7	12	2	460	103*	-	4	1	46.00	7	-	60	1	36	-	-	-	-	-
1995-96	Zimbabwe	1	2	-	34	30	-	-	-	17.00	-	-	-	-	-	-	-	-	-	-
1995-96		8	13	3	681	131*	1	2	3	68.10	7	-	126	4	93	2	46.50	-	-	1/8
1996-97	India	2	4	1	122	58	-	1	-	40.67	3	-	-	-	-	-	-	-	-	-
1996-97		10	18	2	960	159	-	4	3	60.00	10	-	107	5	53	1	53.00	-	-	1/0
1997	England	8	12	3	571	127	-	2	2	63.44	7	-	18	-	9	-	-	-	-	-
1997-98		9	15	4	697	129*	-	2	3	63.36	5	-	30	2	15	-	-	-	-	-
1997-98	India	6	9	-	364	155	-	2	1	40.44	7	-	-	-	-	-	-	-	-	-
Total		82	138	18	6427	211	1	28	22	53.56	70	-	597	19	360	5	72.00	-	-	1/0
Test Cricket		18	29	1	1043	127	-	6	2	37.25	17	-	35	3	8	2	4.00	-	-	1/0
Sheffield Shield		40	73	10	3860	211	1	12	16	61.27	28	-	450	15	274	3	91.33	-	-	1/7

Opponents	M	Inn	NO	Runs	HS	0s	50	100	Avrge	Ct	St	Balls	Mdns	Runs	Wkts	Avrge	5	10	Best
Derbyshire	1	2	-	70	64	-	1	-	35.00	2	-	12	-	7	-	-	-	-	-
England 'A'	1	1	-	1	1	-	-	-	1.00	-	-	4	-	8	-	-	-	-	-
ENGLAND	3	5	-	241	127	-	1	1	48.20	1	-	-	-	-	-	-	-	-	-
England XI	1	1	-	71	71	-	1	-	71.00	-	-	-	-	-	-	-	-	-	-
Glamorgan	2	4	2	189	126*	-	-	1	94.50	1	-	18	-	9	-	-	-	-	-
Guyana	1	1	-	19	19	-	-	-	19.00	1	-	-	-	-	-	-	-	-	-
Hampshire	1	1	-	87	87	-	1	-	87.00	1	-	42	-	29	-	-	-	-	-
Indian Board President's XI	2	3	1	250	155	-	1	1	125.00	1	-	-	-	-	-	-	-	-	-
India 'A'	1	1	-	14	14	-	-	-	14.00	2	-	-	-	-	-	-	-	-	-
INDIA	4	7	-	132	60	-	1	-	18.86	6	-	-	-	-	-	-	-	-	-
Kent	1	2	1	88	56*	-	1	-	88.00	4	-	-	-	-	-	-	-	-	-
Leicestershire	2	3	-	69	64	-	1	-	23.00	2	-	-	-	-	-	-	-	-	-
Middlesex	1	1	-	5	5	-	-	-	5.00	-	-	-	-	-	-	-	-	-	-
NEW ZEALAND	1	2	-	90	53	-	1	-	45.00	1	-	-	-	-	-	-	-	-	-
Nottinghamshire	3	4	1	119	73*	-	1	-	39.67	2	-	-	-	-	-	-	-	-	-
New South Wales	1	1	-	19	19	-	-	-	19.00	-	-	-	-	-	-	-	-	-	-
New Zealanders	9	18	-	748	134	-	3	2	41.56	11	-	72	1	67	1	67.00	-	-	1/39
Pakistanis	1	2	-	69	54	-	1	-	34.50	3	-	-	-	-	-	-	-	-	-
Queensland	1	1	-	35	35	-	-	-	35.00	4	-	24	-	24	-	-	-	-	-
South Australia	7	13	2	745	159	-	1	4	67.73	6	-	90	3	54	-	-	-	-	-
SRI LANKA	9	16	2	971	161	-	4	4	69.36	6	-	120	7	54	1	54.00	-	-	1/7
SOUTH AFRICA	3	4	-	193	96	-	2	-	48.25	4	-	24	2	8	1	8.00	-	-	1/8
Sri Lankans	3	5	-	248	105	-	1	1	49.60	2	-	-	-	-	-	-	-	-	-
Somerset	1	1	1	131	131*	-	-	1	-	-	-	6	-	1	-	-	-	-	-
TCCB XI	1	2	1	106	54	-	2	-	106.00	1	-	-	-	-	-	-	-	-	-
	1	1	-	24	24	-	-	-	24.00	1	-	-	-	-	-	-	-	-	-

	Inn	NO	Runs	HS	Os	50	100	Avrge	Ct	St	Balls	Mdns	Runs	Wkts	Avrge	5	10	Best
Victoria	6	3	479	94*	-	3	-	53.22	2	-	48	2	30	-	-	-	-	-
Western Australia	5	3	917	211	1	1	6	83.36	3	-	120	2	69	1	69.00	-	-	1/32
WEST INDIES	2	-	110	88	-	1	-	27.50	2	-	11	1	0	1	0.00	-	-	1/0
Worcestershire	1	2	133	103*	-	-	1	133.00	1	-	6	1	0	-	-	-	-	-
Zimbabweans	1	2	20	18	-	-	-	10.00	-	-	-	-	-	-	-	-	-	-
Zimbabwe President's XI	1	2	34	30	-	-	-	17.00	-	-	-	-	-	-	-	-	-	-

	Inn	NO	Runs	HS	Os	50	100	Avrge	Ct	St	Balls	Mdns	Runs	Wkts	Avrge	5	10	Best
First Innings	39	4	2198	211	-	12	8	62.80	14	-	125	4	67	2	33.50	-	-	1/0
Second Innings	42	2	1961	155	1	6	8	49.03	20	-	210	9	120	2	60.00	-	-	1/32
Third Innings	31	8	1069	121	1	6	2	46.48	9	-	48	1	29	-	-	-	-	-
Fourth Innings	26	4	1199	161	-	4	4	54.50	27	-	214	5	144	1	144.00	-	-	1/7

Venue	M	Inn	NO	Runs	HS	Os	50	100	Avrge	Ct	St	Balls	Mdns	Runs	Wkts	Avrge	5	10	Best
in Australia																			
Adelaide	7	13	1	604	161	-	2	2	50.33	3	-	48	3	25	-	-	-	-	-
Brisbane	5	9	1	435	119	-	3	1	54.38	3	-	53	2	30	1	30.00	-	-	1/0
Devonport	1	2	-	20	18	-	-	-	10.00	-	-	-	-	-	-	-	-	-	-
Hobart (Bel)	24	42	7	2271	211	1	5	11	64.89	21	-	264	9	174	2	87.00	-	-	1/7
Launceston	3	4	1	201	131*	-	1	1	67.00	3	-	10	-	9	-	-	-	-	-
Melbourne	5	9	2	488	105	-	3	1	69.71	3	-	42	2	23	1	23.00	-	-	1/8
Perth	5	6	-	341	101	-	2	1	56.83	3	-	96	2	51	1	51.00	-	-	1/32
Sydney	7	13	-	497	125	-	3	1	38.23	9	-	6	-	3	-	-	-	-	-
in England																			
Birmingham	1	1	-	24	24	-	-	-	24.00	1	-	-	-	-	-	-	-	-	-
Canterbury	1	2	1	88	56*	-	1	-	88.00	4	-	-	-	-	-	-	-	-	-
Cardiff	1	2	2	154	126*	-	-	1	-	-	-	18	-	9	-	-	-	-	-

Chesterfield	1	2	–	70	64	–	1	–	–	–	–
Leeds	1	1	–	127	127	–	–	35.00	2	12	7
Leicester	2	3	–	69	64	–	1	127.00	1	–	–
Lord's	1	1	–	5	5	–	–	23.00	2	–	–
Neath	1	2	–	35	31	–	–	5.00	–	–	–
Nottingham	2	3	–	73	45	–	–	17.50	1	–	–
Southampton	1	1	–	87	87	–	1	24.33	–	42	29
Taunton	1	2	1	106	54	–	2	87.00	1	–	–
The Oval	1	2	–	60	40	–	–	106.00	1	–	–
Worcester	1	2	1	133	103*	–	1	30.00	–	6	0
in India								133.00	1		
Bangalore	1	1	–	16	16	–	–	16.00	2	–	–
Calcutta	1	2	–	69	60	–	1	34.50	–	–	–
Chennai (Chpk)	1	2	–	20	18	–	–	10.00	1	–	–
Delhi (FSK)	1	2	–	27	14	–	–	13.50	3	–	–
Jamshedpur	1	1	–	14	14	–	–	14.00	2	–	–
Mumbai (BS)	1	2	–	90	53	–	1	45.00	1	–	–
Patiala	1	2	1	95	58	–	1	95.00	–	–	–
Visakhapatnam	1	1	–	155	155	–	1	155.00	1	–	–
in West Indies											
Georgetown	1	1	–	19	19	–	–	19.00	1	–	–
in Zimbabwe											
Bulawayo (QSC)	1	2	–	34	30	–	–	17.00	–	–	–

Country	M	Inn	NO	Runs	HS	0s	50	100	Avrge	Ct	St	Balls	Mdns	Runs	Wkts	Avrge	5	10	Best
Australia	57	98	12	4857	211	1	19	18	56.48	45	-	519	18	315	5	63.00	-	-	1/0
England	15	24	5	1031	127	-	6	3	54.26	14	-	78	1	45	-	-	-	-	-
India	8	13	1	486	155	-	3	1	40.50	10	-	-	-	-	-	-	-	-	-
West Indies	1	1	-	19	19	-	-	-	19.00	1	-	-	-	-	-	-	-	-	-
Zimbabwe	1	2	-	34	30	-	-	-	17.00	-	-	-	-	-	-	-	-	-	-

Batting Position	Inn	NO	Runs	HS	0s	50	100	Avrge
1/2	2	-	60	54	-	1	-	30.00
3	11	1	470	155	-	3	1	47.00
4	88	13	4532	211	1	15	19	60.43
5	10	1	384	96	-	4	-	42.67
6	22	-	848	127	-	4	2	38.55
7	4	2	105	73*	-	1	-	52.50
9	1	1	28	28*	-	-	-	-

Team	M	Inn	NO	Runs	HS	0s	50	100	Avrge	Ct	St	Balls	Mdns	Runs	Wkts	Avrge	5	10	Best
AUSTRALIA	18	29	1	1043	127	-	6	2	37.25	17	-	35	3	8	2	4.00	-	-	1/0
Australian XI	11	15	4	774	155	-	5	2	70.36	11	-	18	-	9	-	-	-	-	-
Tasmania	46	82	11	4150	211	1	13	17	58.45	35	-	484	15	307	3	102.33	-	-	1/7
Young Australians	7	12	2	460	103*	-	4	1	46.00	7	-	60	1	36	-	-	-	-	-

How Dismissed:	Inns	NO	Bwd	Cgt	LBW	Stp	RO	HW	HB
	138	18	19	84	13	3	-	1	

Wickets Taken: Wkts Bwd Cgt C&B LBW Stp HW
                 5   1   3   -   1   -   -

Batsmen Dismissed: Wkts 1/2 3 4 5 6 7 8 9 10 11
                    5   - 2 1 1 1 1 - - - -

Highest Score: 211* Tasmania v Western Australia, Hobart (Bel), 1994-95

100s	Team	Opponent	Venue	Season
125*	Tasmania	New South Wales	Sydney	1992–93
107	Tasmania	Western Australia	Hobart	1992–93
100*	Tasmania	Western Australia	Hobart	1992–93
105	Tasmania	Western Australia	Hobart	1993–94
101	Tasmania	Western Australia	Perth	1993–94
161	Tasmania	South Australia	Adelaide	1993–94
119	Tasmania	Queensland	Brisbane	1994–95
211	Tasmania	Western Australia	Hobart	1994–95
134	Tasmania	New South Wales	Hobart	1994–95
103*	Young Australians	Worcestershire	Worcester	1995
118*	Tasmania	Queensland	Hobart	1995–96
100*	Tasmania	Queensland	Hobart	1995–96
131*	Tasmania	Sri Lankans	Launceston	1995–96
126	Tasmania	South Australia	Hobart	1996–97
145*	Tasmania	South Australia	Hobart	1996–97
159	Tasmania	Queensland	Hobart	1996–97
126*	Australian XI	Glamorgan	Cardiff	1997
127	AUSTRALIA	ENGLAND	Leeds	1997

121	Tasmania	South Australia	Adelaide	1997-98
129*	Tasmania	Western Australia	Hobart	1997-98
105	AUSTRALIA	SOUTH AFRICA	Melbourne	1997-98
155	Australian XI	Indian Board President's XI	Visakhapatnam	1997-98

Best Bowling: 1/0 Australia v West Indies, Brisbane, 1996-97

Batting—Innings by Innings

Gme	Inn	Date	Team	Opp	Venue	Inn	Pos	HO	Fielder	Runs	Bowler	Ttl	Avrge	Ct	St
1992-93 in Australia
1	1	20/11/1992	TAS	SA	Adelaide	2	4	CGT	TJ Nielsen	56	DJ Hickey	56	56.00	-	-
1	2	20/11/1992	TAS	SA	Adelaide	4	4	BWD		4	DJ Hickey	60	30.00	-	-
2	3	27/11/1992	TAS	NSW	Hobart	1	4	CGT	SM Small	32	DA Freedman	92	30.67	-	-
2	4	27/11/1992	TAS	NSW	Hobart	3	6	BWD		18	WJ Holdsworth	110	27.50	-	-
3	5	18/12/1992	TAS	WA	Perth	2	4	LBW		25	PA Capes	135	27.00	-	-
3	5	18/12/1992	TAS	WA	Perth	4	4			-		135	27.00	-	-
4	6	31/12/1992	TAS	VIC	Hobart	2	4	CGT	DS Berry	6	ND Maxwell	141	23.50	-	-
4	7	31/12/1992	TAS	VIC	Hobart	4	4	CGT	DS Berry	41	AIC Dodemaide	182	26.00	-	-
5	8	15/01/1993	TAS	SA	Hobart	1	4	CGT	TJ Nielsen	50	DA Reeves	232	29.00	-	-
5	8	15/01/1993	TAS	SA	Hobart	4	4			-		232	29.00	1	-
6	9	21/01/1993	TAS	QLD	Brisbane	2	4	CGT	ML Hayden	11	CG Rackemann	243	27.00	-	-
6	9	21/01/1993	TAS	QLD	Brisbane	4	4			-		243	27.00	1	-
7	10	27/01/1993	TAS	NSW	Sydney	1	4	CGT	SM Small	125	WJ Holdsworth	368	36.80	1	-
7	11	27/01/1993	TAS	NSW	Sydney	3	4	CGT	SM Small	69	GRJ Matthews	437	39.73	-	-
8	11	08/02/1993	TAS	ENA	Launceston	2	4			-		437	39.73	-	-
8	12	08/02/1993	TAS	ENA	Launceston	4	4	LBW		1	J Boiling	438	36.50	-	-
9	13	26/02/1993	TAS	VIC	Melbourne	2	4	HW		34	JA Sutherland	472	36.31	1	-

9	14	26/02/1993	TAS	VIC	Melbourne	4	CGT	AIC Dodemaide	C Howard	64	536	38.29	–
10	15	11/03/1993	TAS	WA	Hobart	2	CGT	TJ Zoehrer	J Angel	107	643	42.87	–
10	16	11/03/1993	TAS	WA	Hobart	4	NO			100*	743	49.53	2
11	17	18/03/1993	TAS	QLD	Hobart	2	CGT	SG Law	CJ Rowell	12	755	47.19	2
11	18	18/03/1993	TAS	QLD	Hobart	4	CGT	MS Kasprowicz	GJ Rowell	27	782	46.00	1

1993–94 in Australia

12	19	04/11/1993	TAS	NZS	Launceston	1	CGT	BA Pocock	W Watson	15	797	44.28	1
12	20	04/11/1993	TAS	NZS	Launceston	3	CGT	BA Pocock	W Watson	54	851	44.79	2
13	21	11/11/1993	TAS	WA	Hobart	2	LBW		J Angel	105	956	47.80	–
13	21	11/11/1993	TAS	WA	Hobart	4				–	956	47.80	–
14	22	25/11/1993	TAS	NSW	Sydney	2	CGT	RJ Davison	GRJ Matthews	15	971	46.24	–
14	23	25/11/1993	TAS	NSW	Sydney	4	BWD		GRJ Matthews	35	1006	45.73	3
15	24	10/12/1993	TAS	VIC	Hobart	1	CGT	DJ Ramshaw	DW Fleming	23	1029	44.74	–
15	25	10/12/1993	TAS	VIC	Hobart	3	BWD		C Howard	66	1095	45.63	–
16	26	31/12/1993	TAS	QLD	Brisbane	2	CGT	WA Seccombe	CG Rackemann	12	1107	44.28	–
16	27	31/12/1993	TAS	QLD	Brisbane	4	STP	WA Seccombe	PW Jackson	64	1171	45.04	–
17	28	07/01/1994	TAS	NSW	Hobart	2	CGT	WJ Holdsworth	PJS Alley	3	1174	43.48	2
17	29	07/01/1994	TAS	NSW	Hobart	4	CGT	WJ Holdsworth	GR Robertson	13	1187	42.39	–
18	30	18/01/1994	TAS	SA	Hobart	2	CGT	DS Lehmann	SP George	16	1203	41.48	–
18	31	18/01/1994	TAS	SA	Hobart	4	CGT	PC Nobes	DJ Marsh	40	1243	41.43	1
19	32	10/02/1994	TAS	QLD	Hobart	2	BWD		D Tazelaar	49	1292	41.68	–
19	33	10/02/1994	TAS	QLD	Hobart	4	CGT	WA Seccombe	CG Rackemann	18	1310	40.94	–
20	34	17/02/1994	TAS	VIC	Melbourne	1	CGT	DS Berry	SH Cook	42	1352	40.97	1
20	35	17/02/1994	TAS	VIC	Melbourne	3	NO			20*	1372	41.58	–
21	36	24/02/1994	TAS	WA	Perth	2	CGT	DJ Spencer	J Angel	101	1473	43.32	–
21	36	24/02/1994	TAS	WA	Perth	5				–	1473	43.32	–

22	37	17/03/1994	TAS	SA	Adelaide	2	4	NO	PE McIntyre	84*	1557	45.79	1	-
22	38	17/03/1994	TAS	SA	Adelaide	4	4	CGT	JD Siddons	BE McNamara	161	1718	49.09	-	-
23	39	25/03/1994	TAS	NSW	Sydney	1	4	BWD		1	1719	47.75	2	-
23	40	25/03/1994	TAS	NEW	Sydney	3	4	CGT	RJ Davison	PJS Alley	28	1747	47.22	-	-

1994–95 in Australia

24	41	13/10/1994	TAS	QLD	Brisbane	2	4	BWD		GJ Rowell	119	1866	49.11	-	-
24	42	13/10/1994	TAS	QLD	Brisbane	4	4	CGT	GJ Rowell	AR Border	33	1899	48.69	-	-
25	43	19/10/1994	TAS	SA	Adelaide	1	4	LBW		MJP Minagall	45	1944	48.60	-	-
25	44	19/10/1994	TAS	SA	Adelaide	3	4	LBW		MA Harrity	16	1960	47.80	-	-
26	45	04/11/1994	TAS	WA	Hobart	1	4	CGT	MP Lavender	J Stewart	211	2171	51.69	-	-
27	46	18/11/1994	AXI	EXI	Hobart	1	5	CGT	SJ Rhodes	MJ McCague	71	2242	52.14	-	-
27	46	18/11/1994	AXI	EXI	Hobart	4	5				-	2242	52.14	-	-
28	47	18/12/1994	TAS	ZMS	Devonport	1	5	CGT	IP Butchart	HH Streak	2	2244	51.00	-	-
28	48	18/12/1994	TAS	ZMS	Devonport	3	4	STP	A Flower	SG Peall	18	2262	50.27	-	-
29	49	20/01/1995	TAS	NSW	Hobart	2	4	BWD		SM Thompson	58	2320	50.43	-	-
29	50	20/01/1995	TAS	NSW	Hobart	4	4	CGT	AJ Kershler	SM Thompson	134	2454	52.21	1	-
30	51	27/01/1995	TAS	SA	Hobart	2	4	CGT	JD Siddons	SP George	62	2516	52.42	-	-
30	52	27/01/1995	TAS	SA	Hobart	4	4	CGT	JD Siddons	BA Johnson	3	2519	51.41	-	-

1994–95 in West Indies

31	53	20/03/1995	AXI	GUY	Georgetown	2	5	CGT	PD Persaud	LA Joseph	19	2538	50.76	-	-
31	53	20/03/1995	AXI	GUY	Georgetown	4	5				-	2538	50.76	1	-

1995 in England

32	54	05/07/1995	YAU	SOM	Taunton	1	2	C&B	GD Rose	GD Rose	54	2592	50.82	-	-
32	55	05/07/1995	YAU	SOM	Taunton	3	4	NO			52*	2644	51.84	1	-

33	56	08/07/1995	YAU	GLA	Neath	2	4	LBW		AD Dale	4	2648	50.92	1	-
33	57	08/07/1995	YAU	GLA	Neath	4	4	CGT	AJ Dalton	NM Kendrick	31	2679	50.55	-	-
34	58	19/07/1995	YAU	DER	Chesterfield	2	2	CGT	DG Cork	DE Malcolm	6	2685	49.72	1	-
34	59	19/07/1995	YAU	DER	Chesterfield	4	4	CGT	CJ Adams	TA Tweats	64	2749	49.98	1	-
35	60	22/07/1995	YAU	WOR	Worcester	2	4	NO			103*	2852	51.85	1	-
35	61	22/07/1995	YAU	WOR	Worcester	4	4	CGT	TM Moody	SR Lampitt	30	2882	51.46	-	-
36	62	28/07/1995	YAU	HAM	Southampton	1	6	LBW		SD Udal	87	2969	52.09	1	-
36	62	28/07/1995	YAU	HAM	Southampton	4	6				-	2969	52.09	-	-
37	63	03/08/1995	YAU	LEI	Leicester	1	4	CGT	IJ Sutcliffe	A Sheriyar	4	2973	51.26	-	-
37	64	03/08/1995	YAU	LEI	Leicester	3	4	CGT	PA Nixon	A Sheriyar	1	2974	50.41	-	-
38	65	17/08/1995	YAU	TCC	Birmingham	2	4	BWD		RDB Croft	24	2998	49.97	1	-
38	65	17/08/1995	YAU	TCC	Birmingham	4	4				-	2998	49.97	-	-

1995–96 in Zimbabwe

39	66	09/10/1995	TAS	ZXI	Bulawayo	1	4	CGT	CB Wishart	ACI Lock	30	3028	49.64	-	-
39	67	09/10/1995	TAS	ZXI	Bulawayo	3	4	CGT	(S)J Laney	M Mbangwa	4	3032	48.90	-	-

1995–96 in Australia

40	68	26/10/1995	TAS	NSW	Sydney	2	4	LBW		DA Freedman	20	3052	48.44	1	-
40	69	26/10/1995	TAS	NSW	Sydney	4	4	LBW		GD McGrath	43	3095	48.36	-	-
41	70	02/11/1995	TAS	QLD	Hobart	1	4	NO			118*	3213	50.20	-	-
41	71	02/11/1995	TAS	QLD	Hobart	3	4	NO			100*	3313	51.77	-	-
42	72	24/11/1995	TAS	NSW	Hobart	2	4	CGT	KJ Roberts	ND Maxwell	46	3359	51.68	-	-
42	73	24/11/1995	TAS	NSW	Hobart	4	4	CGT	SM Thompson	GRJ Matthews	22	3381	51.23	1	-
43	74	01/12/1995	TAS	SLS	Launceston	1	4	NO			131*	3512	53.21	-	-
43	74	01/12/1995	TAS	SLS	Launceston	3	8				-	3512	53.21	-	-
44	75	08/12/1995	AUS	SL	Perth	2	5	LBW		WPUJC Vaas	96	3608	53.85	-	-

44	75	08/12/1995	AUS	SL	Perth	4	5			-	3608	53.85	3	-
45	76	26/12/1995	AUS	SL	Melbourne	1	6	CGT	AP Gurinsinha	71	3679	54.10	-	-
45	76	26/12/1995	AUS	SL	Melbourne	4	6			-	3679	54.10	1	-
46	77	25/01/1996	AUS	SL	Adelaide	1	6	CGT	RS Kaluwitharana	6	3685	53.41	-	-
46	78	25/01/1996	AUS	SL	Adelaide	3	6	CGT	RS Kaluwitharana	20	3705	52.93	-	-
47	79	23/03/1996	TAS	WA	Hobart	1	4	CGT	AC Gilchrist	8	3713	52.30	-	-
47	80	23/03/1996	TAS	WA	Hobart	3	4	CGT	AC Gilchrist	0	3713	51.57	1	-

1996–97 in India

48	81	05/10/1996	AXI	IBP	Patiala	1	3	CGT	P Dharmani	58	3771	51.66	-	-
48	82	05/10/1996	AXI	IBP	Patiala	3	3	NO		37*	3808	52.16	-	-
49	83	10/10/1996	AUS	IND	Delhi	1	3	BWD	AR Kapoor	14	3822	51.65	3	-
49	84	10/10/1996	AUS	IND	Delhi	3	3	BWD	VBK Prasad	13	3835	51.13	-	-

1996–97 in Australia

50	85	15/11/1996	TAS	WA	Perth	1	4	CGT	RJ Campbell	RM Baker	67	3902	51.34	-	-
50	86	15/11/1996	TAS	WA	Perth	3	4	STP	RJ Campbell	TM Moody	36	3938	51.14	-	-
51	87	22/11/1996	AUS	WI	Brisbane	1	3	CGT	CA Walsh	KCG Benjamin	88	4026	51.62	1	-
51	88	22/11/1966	AUS	WI	Brisbane	3	3	CGT	CP Browne	IR Bishop	9	4035	51.08	1	-
52	89	29/11/1996	AUS	WI	Sydney	1	3	CGT	RG Samuels	CA Walsh	9	4044	50.55	-	-
52	90	29/11/1996	AUS	WI	Sydney	3	3	CGT	CO Browne	IR Bishop	4	4048	49.98	-	-
53	91	19/12/1995	TAS	PKI	Hobart	2	4	C&B	Mohammad Zahid	Mohammad Zahid	35	4083	49.79	3	-
53	91	19/12/1956	TAS	PKI	Hobart	4	4			-	4083	49.79	1	-
54	92	09/01/1997	TAS	VIC	Melbourne	1	4	CGT	DS Berry	AIC Dodemaide	26	4109	49.51	-	-
54	93	09/01/1937	TAS	VIC	Melbourne	3	4	NO		94*	4203	50.64	-	-
55	94	24/01/1997	TAS	WA	Hobart	1	4	CGT	RJ Campbell	J Angel	8	4211	50.13	-	-
55	95	24/01/1997	TAS	WA	Hobart	3	4	BWD		TM Moody	6	4217	49.61	-	-

56	96	01/02/1997	TAS	SA	Adelaide	2	4	CGT	TJ Nielsen	SP George	39	4256	49.49	-
56	96	01/02/1997	TAS	SA	Adelaide	4	4				-	4256	49.49	1
57	97	11/02/1997	TAS	SA	Hobart	2	4	BWD		JC Scuderi	126	4382	50.37	1
57	98	11/02/1997	TAS	SA	Hobart	4	4	NO			145*	4527	52.03	-
58	99	07/03/1997	TAS	QLD	Hobart	1	4	CGT	MP Mott	BN Creevey	159	4686	53.25	2
58	100	07/03/1997	TAS	QLD	Hobart	3	4	CGT	SG Law	PW Jackson	23	4709	52.91	-
59	101	13/03/1997	TAS	NSW	Sydney	1	4	CGT	PA Emery	S Lee	64	4773	53.03	-
59	102	13/03/1997	TAS	NSW	Sydney	3	4	CGT	KJ Roberts	SCG MacGill	22	4795	52.69	-

1997 in England

60	103	11/06/1997	AXI	NOT	Nottingham	2	3	LBW		RA Pick	19	4814	52.33	-
61	104	14/06/1997	AXI	LEI	Leicester	1	3	BWD		J Ormond	64	4878	52.45	-
61	104	14/06/1997	AXI	LEI	Leicester	3	5				-	4878	52.45	2
62	105	16/07/1997	AXI	GLA	Cardiff	1	4	NO			126*	5004	53.81	-
62	106	16/07/1997	AXI	GLA	Cardiff	3	9	NO			28*	5032	54.11	-
63	107	19/07/1997	AXI	MID	Lord's	2	6	CGT	OA Shah	PCR Tufnell	5	5037	53.59	-
63	107	19/07/1997	AXI	MID	Lord's	4	6				-	5037	53.59	-
64	108	24/07/1997	AUS	ENG	Leeds	2	6	CGT	MA Ealham	D Gough	127	5164	54.36	1
64	108	24/07/1997	AUS	ENG	Leeds	4	6				-	5164	54.36	-
65	109	07/08/1997	AUS	ENG	Nottingham	1	6	BWD		DW Headley	9	5173	53.89	-
65	110	07/08/1997	AUS	ENG	Nottingham	3	6	CGT	AJ Stewart	AJ Hollioake	45	5218	53.79	-
66	111	16/08/1997	AXI	KEN	Canterbury	2	6	BWD		MA Ealham	32	5250	53.57	1
66	112	16/08/1997	AXI	KEN	Canterbury	4	5	NO			56*	5306	54.14	3
67	113	21/08/1997	AUS	ENG	The Oval	2	6	CGT	N Hussain	PCR Tufnell	40	5346	54.00	-
67	114	21/08/1997	AUS	ENG	The Oval	4	6	LBW		PCR Tufnell	20	5366	54.66	-

1997–98 in Australia

68	115	15/10/1997	TAS	SA	Adelaide	1	4	CGT	TJ Nielsen		3	5369	53.16	1
68	116	15/10/1997	TAS	SA	Adelaide	3	4	CGT	DS Lehmann		121	5490	53.82	-
69	117	31/10/1997	TAS	WA	Hobart	1	4	NO			129*	5619	55.09	-
69	118	31/10/1997	TAS	WA	Hobart	3	7	NO			14*	5633	55.23	-
70	119	07/11/1997	AUS	NZ	Brisbane	1	6	CGT	BA Pocock	SB Doull	26	5659	54.94	-
70	120	07/11/1997	AUS	NZ	Brisbane	3	7	NO			73*	5732	55.65	-
71	121	20/11/1997	AUS	NZ	Perth	2	7	CGT	SP Fleming	CL Cairns	16	5748	55.27	-
71	121	20/11/1997	AUS	NZ	Perth	4	6				-	5748	55.27	-
72	122	27/11/1997	AUS	NZ	Hobart	1	6	CGT	AC Parore	CL Cairns	4	5752	54.78	-
72	122	27/11/1997	AUS	NZ	Hobart	3	6				-	5752	54.78	2
73	123	19/12/1997	TAS	VIC	Hobart	2	4	CGT	GR Vimpani	DJ Saker	38	5790	54.62	-
73	124	19/12/1997	TAS	VIC	Hobart	4	4	NO			25*	5815	54.86	-
74	125	26/12/1997	AUS	SAF	Melbourne	1	6	BWD		PL Symcox	105	5920	55.33	-
74	126	26/12/1997	AUS	SAF	Melbourne	3	6	C&B	SM Pollock	SM Pollock	32	5952	55.11	-
75	127	02/01/1998	AUS	SAF	Sydney	2	6	C&B	PR Adams	PR Adams	62	6014	55.17	-
75	127	02/01/1998	AUS	SAF	Sydney	4	6				-	6014	55.17	2
76	128	30/01/1998	AUS	SAF	Adelaide	2	6	BWD		L Klusener	26	6040	54.91	-
76	129	30/01/1998	AUS	SAF	Adelaide	4	6	CGT	PL Symcox	L Klusener	23	6063	54.62	-

1997–98 in India

77	130	24/02/1998	AXI	MUM	Mumbai	1	4	CGT	AA Muzumdar	NM Kulkarni	53	6116	54.61	1
77	131	24/02/1998	AXI	MUM	Mumbai	3	5	CGT	SK Kulkarni	NM Kulkarni	37	6153	54.45	-
78	132	01/03/1998	AXI	IBP	Visakhapatnam	2	3	CGT	SS Karim	A Kuruvilla	155	6308	55.33	1
79	133	06/03/1998	AUS	IND	Chennai	2	5	CGT	NR Mongia	SLV Raju	18	6326	55.01	-
79	134	06/03/1998	AUS	IND	Chennai	4	7	LBW		SLV Raju	2	6328	54.55	1
80	135	13/03/1998	AXI	INA	Jamshedpur	2	6	CGT	V Rathore	KN Ananthapadmanabha	14	6342	54.21	2

80	135	13/03/1998	AXI	INA	Jamshedpur	4	2	7	6	BWD			-	6342	54.21	-	-
81	136	18/03/1998	AUS	IND	Calcutta	1	-	3	6	BWD			60	6402	54.25	-	-
81	137	18/03/1998	AUS	IND	Calcutta	3	-	3	5	CGT	J Srinath	AR Kumble	9	6411	53.87	-	-
82	138	25/03/1998	AUS	IND	Bangalore	2	-	6	6	CGT	SR Tendulkar	AR Kumble	16	6427	53.56	1	1
82	138	25/03/1998	AUS	IND	Bangalore	4	-	8	6			AR Kumble	-	6427	53.56	1	1

Bowling—Innings by Innings

Game	Date	Team	Opp	Venue	Ovrs	Md	Rns	Wk	Balls	Mdns	Runs	Wkts	Avrge	5wi	10m	Stk/Rt
1992–93 in Australia																
3	18/12/1992	TAS	WA	Perth	6.0	2	7	-	36	2	7	-	-	-	-	-
3	18/12/1992	TAS	WA	Perth	1.0	-	3	-	42	2	10	-	-	-	-	-
5	15/01/1993	TAS	SA	Hobart	1.0	-	6	-	48	2	16	-	-	-	-	-
8	08/02/1993	TAS	ENA	Launceston	0.4	-	8	-	52	2	24	-	-	-	-	-
1993/94 in Australia																
13	11/11/1993	TAS	WA	Hobart	1.0	-	1	-	58	2	25	-	-	-	-	-
16	31/12/1993	TAS	QLD	Brisbane	7.0	1	30	-	100	3	55	-	-	-	-	-
18	18/01/1994	TAS	SA	Hobart	3.0	1	7	1	118	4	62	1	62.00	-	-	118.00
21	24/02/1994	TAS	WA	Perth	7.0	-	32	1	160	4	94	2	47.00	-	-	80.00
22	17/03/1994	TAS	SA	Adelaide	6.0	3	15	-	196	7	109	2	54.50	-	-	98.00
23	25/03/1994	TAS	NSW	Sydney	1.0	-	3	-	202	7	112	2	56.00	-	-	101.00
1994/95 in Australia																
25	19/10/1994	TAS	SA	Adelaide	2.0	-	10	-	214	7	122	2	61.00	-	-	107.00
29	20/01/1995	TAS	NSW	Hobart	3.0	-	17	-	232	7	139	2	69.50	-	-	116.00
30	27/01/1995	TAS	SA	Hobart	2.0	-	3	-	244	7	142	2	71.00	-	-	122.00
30	27/01/1995	TAS	SA	Hobart	2.0	-	12	-	256	7	154	2	77.00	-	-	128.00

1995 in England

34	19/07/1995	YAU	DER	Chesterfield	2.0	-	7	-	268	7	161	2	80.50	-	134.00
35	22/07/1995	YAU	WOR	Worcester	1.0	1	0	-	274	8	161	2	80.50	-	137.00
36	28/07/1995	YAU	HAM	Southampton	7.0	-	29	-	316	8	190	2	95.00	-	158.00

1995/96 in Australia

41	02/11/1995	TAS	QLD	Hobart	5.0	1	20	-	346	9	210	2	105.00	-	173.00
42	24/11/1995	TAS	NSW	Hobart	7.0	1	39	1	388	10	249	3	83.00	-	129.33
42	24/11/1995	TAS	NSW	Hobart	1.0	-	8	-	394	10	257	3	85.67	-	131.33
43	01/12/1995	TAS	SLS	Launceston	1.0	-	1	-	400	10	258	3	86.00	-	133.33
45	26/12/1995	AUS	SL	Melbourne	4.0	2	8	1	424	12	266	4	66.50	-	106.00
47	23/03/1996	TAS	WA	Hobart	3.0	-	17	-	442	12	283	4	70.75	-	110.50

1996/97 in Australia

50	15/11/1996	TAS	WA	Perth	2.0	-	9	-	454	12	292	4	73.00	-	113.50
51	22/11/1996	AUS	WI	Brisbane	1.5	1	0	1	465	13	292	5	58.40	-	93.00
53	19/12/1996	TAS	PKI	Hobart	4.0	-	24	-	489	13	316	5	63.20	-	97.80
54	09/01/1997	TAS	VIC	Melbourne	3.0	-	15	-	507	13	331	5	66.20	-	101.40
57	11/02/1997	TAS	SA	Hobart	2.0	2	0	-	519	15	331	5	66.20	-	103.80
57	11/02/1997	TAS	SA	Hobart	2.0	1	1	-	531	16	332	5	66.40	-	106.20
58	07/03/1997	TAS	QLD	Hobart	3.0	1	4	-	549	17	336	5	67.20	-	109.80

1997 in England

62	16/07/1997	AXI	GLA	Cardiff	3.0	-	9	-	567	17	345	5	69.00	-	113.40

1997/98 in Australia

73	19/12/1997	TAS	VIC	Hobart	5.0	2	15	-	597	19	360	5	72.00	-	119.40

Test Career
Debut: 1995-96 Australia v Sri Lanka, Perth

Season	Opponent	Venue	M	Inn	NO	Runs	HS	0s	50	100	Avrge	Ct	St	Balls	Mdns	Runs	Wkts	Avrge	5	10	Best
1995-96	Sri Lanka	Australia	3	4	-	193	96	-	2	-	48.25	4	-	24	2	8	1	8.00	-	-	1/8
1996-97	India	India	1	2	-	27	14	-	-	-	13.50	3	-	-	-	-	-	-	-	-	-
1996-97	West Indies	Australia	2	4	-	110	88	-	1	-	27.50	2	-	11	1	0	1	0.00	-	-	1/0
1997	England	England	3	5	-	241	127	-	1	1	48.20	1	-	-	-	-	-	-	-	-	-
1997-98	New Zealand	Australia	3	4	1	119	73*	-	1	-	39.67	2	-	-	-	-	-	-	-	-	-
1997-98	South Africa	Australia	3	5	-	248	105	-	1	1	49.60	2	-	-	-	-	-	-	-	-	-
1997-98	India	India	3	5	-	105	60	-	1	-	21.00	3	-	-	-	-	-	-	-	-	-
Total			18	29	1	1043	127	-	6	2	37.25	17	-	35	3	8	2	4.00	-	-	1/0

Opponents	M	Inn	NO	Runs	HS	0s	50	100	Avrge	Ct	St	Balls	Mdns	Runs	Wkts	Avrge	5	10	Best
ENGLAND	3	5	-	241	127	-	-	1	48.20	1	-	-	-	-	-	-	-	-	-
INDIA	4	7	-	132	60	-	1	-	18.86	6	-	-	-	-	-	-	-	-	-
NEW ZEALAND	3	4	1	119	73*	-	1	-	39.67	2	-	-	-	-	-	-	-	-	-
SRI LANKA	3	4	-	193	96	-	2	-	48.25	4	-	24	2	8	1	8.00	-	-	1/8
SOUTH AFRICA	3	5	-	248	105	-	1	1	49.60	2	-	-	-	-	-	-	-	-	-
WEST INDIES	2	4	-	110	88	-	1	-	27.50	2	-	11	1	0	1	0.00	-	-	1/0

	Inn	NO	Runs	HS	0s	50	100	Avrge	Ct	St	Balls	Mdns	Runs	Wkts	Avrge	5	10	Best
First Innings	10	-	392	105	-	3	1	39.20	4	-	35	3	8	2	4.00	-	-	1/0
Second Innings	8	-	401	127	-	2	1	50.13	2	-	-	-	-	-	-	-	-	-
Third Innings	8	1	205	73*	-	1	-	29.29	3	-	-	-	-	-	-	-	-	-
Fourth Innings	3	-	45	23	-	-	-	15.00	8	-	-	-	-	-	-	-	-	-

Venue	M	Inn	NO	Runs	HS	Os	50	100	Avrge	Ct	St	Balls	Mdns	Runs	Wkts	Avrge	5	10	Best
in Australia																			
Adelaide	2	4	-	75	26	-	-	-	18.75	-	-	-	-	-	-	-	-	-	-
Brisbane	2	4	1	196	88	-	2	-	65.33	2	-	11	1	0	1	0.00	-	-	1/0
Hobart (Bel)	1	1	-	4	4	-	-	-	4.00	2	-	-	-	-	-	-	-	-	-
Melbourne	2	3	-	208	105	-	1	1	69.33	1	-	24	2	8	1	8.00	-	-	1/8
Perth	2	2	-	112	96	-	1	-	56.00	3	-	-	-	-	-	-	-	-	-
Sydney	2	3	-	75	62	-	1	-	25.00	2	-	-	-	-	-	-	-	-	-
in England																			
Leeds	1	1	-	127	127	-	-	1	127.00	1	-	-	-	-	-	-	-	-	-
Nottingham	1	2	-	54	45	-	-	-	27.00	-	-	-	-	-	-	-	-	-	-
The Oval	1	2	-	60	40	-	-	-	30.00	-	-	-	-	-	-	-	-	-	-
in India																			
Bangalore	1	1	-	16	16	-	-	-	16.00	2	-	-	-	-	-	-	-	-	-
Calcutta	1	2	-	69	60	-	1	-	34.50	-	-	-	-	-	-	-	-	-	-
Chennai (Chpk)	1	2	-	20	18	-	-	-	10.00	1	-	-	-	-	-	-	-	-	-
Delhi (FSK)	1	2	-	27	14	-	-	-	13.50	3	-	-	-	-	-	-	-	-	-

Country	M	Inn	NO	Runs	HS	Os	50	100	Avrge	Ct	St	Balls	Mdns	Runs	Wkts	Avrge	5	10	Best
Australia	11	17	1	670	105	-	5	1	41.88	10	-	35	3	8	2	4.00	-	-	1/0
England	3	5	-	241	127	-	-	1	48.20	1	-	-	-	-	-	-	-	-	-
India	4	7	-	132	60	-	1	-	18.86	6	-	-	-	-	-	-	-	-	-

Batting Position

	Inn	NO	Runs	HS	Os	50	100	Avrge
3	6	-	137	88	-	1	-	22.83
5	3	-	123	96	-	1	-	41.00
6	17	-	692	127	-	3	2	40.71
7	3	1	91	73*	-	1	-	45.50

How Dismissed:

Inns	NO	Bwd	Cgt	LBW	Stp	RO	HW	HB
29	1	6	19	3	-	-	-	-

Wickets Taken:

Wkts	Bwd	Cgt	C&B	LBW	Stp	HW
2	-	1	-	1	-	-

Batsmen Dismissed:

Wkts	1/2	3	4	5	6	7	8	9	10	11
2	-	1	-	-	1	-	-	-	-	-

Highest Score: 127 Australia v England, Leeds, 1997

100s	Team	Opponent	Venue	Season
127	Australia	England	Leeds	1997
105	Australia	South Africa	Melbourne	1997–98

Best Bowling: 1/0 Australia v West Indies, Brisbane, 1996–97

Batting—Innings by Innings

Gme	Inn	Date	Team	Opp	Venue	Inn	Pos	HO	Fielder	Bowler	Runs	Ttl	Avrge	Ct	St
\multicolumn{16}{l}{1995–96 in Australia}
1	1	08/12/1995	AUS	SL	Perth	2	5	LBW		WPUJC Vaas	96	96	96.00	-	-
1	1	08/12/1995	AUS	SL	Perth	4	5				-	96	96.00	3	-
2	2	26/12/1995	AUS	SL	Melbourne	1	6	CGT	AP Gurinsinha	KJ Silva	71	167	83.50	-	-
2	2	26/12/1995	AUS	SL	Melbourne	4	6				-	167	83.50	1	-
3	3	25/01/1996	AUS	SL	Adelaide	1	6	CGT	RS Kaluwitharana	WPUJC Vaas	6	173	57.67	-	-
3	4	25/01/1996	AUS	SL	Adelaide	3	6	CGT	RS Kaluwitharana	WPUJC Vaas	20	193	48.25	-	-
\multicolumn{16}{l}{1996–97 in India}
4	5	10/10/1996	AUS	IND	Delhi	1	3	BWD		AR Kapoor	14	207	41.40	3	-
4	6	10/10/1996	AUS	IND	Delhi	3	3	BWD		VBK Prasad	13	220	36.67	-	-
\multicolumn{16}{l}{1996–97 in Australia}
5	7	22/11/1996	AUS	WI	Brisbane	1	3	CGT	CA Walsh	KCG Benjamin	88	308	44.00	1	-
5	8	22/11/1996	AUS	WI	Brisbane	3	3	CGT	CO Browne	IR Bishop	9	317	39.63	1	-
6	9	29/11/1996	AUS	WI	Sydney	1	3	CGT	RG Samuels	CA Walsh	9	326	36.22	-	-
6	10	29/11/1996	AUS	WI	Sydney	3	3	CGT	CO Browne	IR Bishop	4	330	33.00	-	-
\multicolumn{16}{l}{1997 in England}
7	11	24/07/1997	AUS	ENG	Leeds	2	6	CGT	MA Ealham	D Gough	127	457	41.55	1	-
7	11	24/07/1997	AUS	ENG	Leeds	4	6				-	457	41.55	-	-
8	12	07/08/1997	AUS	ENG	Nottingham	1	6	BWD		DW Headley	9	466	38.83	-	-
8	13	07/08/1997	AUS	ENG	Nottingham	3	6	CGT	AJ Stewart	AJ Hollioake	45	511	39.31	-	-
9	14	21/08/1997	AUS	ENG	The Oval	2	6	CGT	N Hussain	PCR Tufnell	40	551	39.36	-	-
9	15	21/08/1997	AUS	ENG	The Oval	4	6	LBW		PCR Tufnell	20	571	38.07	-	-

1997–98 in Australia

10	16	07/11/1997	AUS	NZ	Brisbane	1	6	CGT	BA Pocock	SB Doull	27	597	37.31	–
10	17	07/11/1997	AUS	NZ	Brisbane	3	7	NO			73*	670	41.88	–
11	18	20/11/1997	AUS	NZ	Perth	2	7	CGT	SP Fleming	CL Cairns	16	686	40.35	–
11	18	20/11/1997	AUS	NZ	Perth	4	6				–	686	40.35	–
12	19	27/11/1997	AUS	NZ	Hobart	1	6	CGT	AC Parore	CL Cairns	4	690	38.33	–
12	19	27/11/1997	AUS	NZ	Hobart	3	6				–	690	38.33	2
13	20	26/12/1997	AUS	SAF	Melbourne	1	6	BWD	SM Pollock	PL Symcox	105	795	41.84	–
13	21	26/12/1997	AUS	SAF	Melbourne	3	6	C&B	SM Pollock	SM Pollock	32	827	41.35	–
14	22	02/01/1998	AUS	SAF	Sydney	2	6	C&B	PR Adams	PR Adams	62	889	42.33	–
14	22	02/01/1998	AUS	SAF	Sydney	4	6				–	889	42.33	2
15	23	30/01/1998	AUS	SAF	Adelaide	2	6	BWD		L Klusener	26	915	41.59	–
15	24	30/01/1998	AUS	SAF	Adelaide	4	6	CGT	PL Symcox	L Klusener	23	938	40.78	–

1997–98 in India

16	25	06/03/1998	AUS	IND	Chennai	2	5	CGT	NR Mongia	SLV Raju	18	956	39.83	–
16	26	06/03/1998	AUS	IND	Chennai	4	7	LBW		SLV Raju	2	958	38.32	1
17	27	18/03/1998	AUS	IND	Calcutta	1	6	BWD		AR Kumble	60	1018	39.15	–
17	28	18/03/1998	AUS	IND	Calcutta	3	5	CGT	J Srinath	AR Kumble	9	1027	38.04	–
18	29	25/03/1998	AUS	IND	Bangalore	2	6	CGT	SR Tendulkar	AR Kumble	16	1043	37.25	1
18	29	25/03/1998	AUS	IND	Bangalore	4	6				–	1043	37.25	1

Bowling—Innings by Innings

Test	Date	Team	Opp	Venue	Ovrs	Md	Rns	Wk	Balls	Mdns	Runs	Wkt	Avrge	5wi	10m	Stk/Rt
1995–96 in Australia																
2	26/12/1995	AUS	SL	Melbourne	4.0	2	8	1	24	2	8	1	8.00	-	-	24.00
1996–97 in Australia																
5	22/11/1996	AUS	WI	Brisbane	1.5	1	0	1	35	3	8	2	4.00	-	-	17.50

International Limited-Over Career

Debut: 1994–95 Australia v South Africa, Wellington

Season			M	Inn	NO	Runs	HS	0s	50	100	Avrge	Stk/Rt	Ct	St
1994–95	NZ Centenary	NZ	4	4	2	80	62	1	1	-	40.00	71.43	-	-
1994–95	WI v Australia	WI	2	2	-	43	43	1	-	-	21.50	61.43	-	-
1995–96	World Series	AUS	10	10	-	341	123	1	3	1	34.10	73.49	2	-
1995–96	World Cup	IPS	7	7	-	229	102	1	-	1	32.71	68.15	1	-
1996–97	Singer World Series	SL	4	4	1	116	53	1	1	-	38.67	69.05	1	-
1996–97	Titan Cup	IND	3	3	-	52	35	1	-	-	17.33	65.00	-	-
1996–97	CUB Series	AUS	3	3	-	68	44	-	-	-	22.67	49.64	-	-
1997–98	CUB Series	AUS	9	9	1	462	100	-	3	1	57.75	75.37	3	-
1997–98	New Zealand v Aust	NZ	4	4	1	76	30	-	-	-	25.33	63.33	1	-
1997–98	Triangular Cup	IND	5	5	-	335	145	-	2	1	67.00	75.96	1	-
1997–98	Coca-Cola Cup	SHJ	4	4	-	132	52	-	1	-	33.00	80.49	1	-
Total			55	55	5	1934	145	5	11	4	38.68	71.50	10	-

Opponents	M	Inn	NO	Runs	HS	0s	50	100	Avrge	Stk/Rt	Ct	St
India	9	9	-	291	84	1	2	-	32.33	71.32	2	-
Kenya	1	1	-	6	6	-	-	-	6.00	42.86	1	-
New Zealand	11	11	4	420	100	-	3	1	60.00	75.40	2	-
Pakistan	1	1	-	19	19	-	-	-	19.00	55.88	-	-
Sri Lanka	9	9	1	371	123	-	2	1	46.38	73.47	1	-
South Africa	10	10	-	271	76	1	1	-	27.10	69.49	2	-
West Indies	10	10	-	272	102	3	1	1	27.20	64.45	1	-
Zimbabwe	4	4	-	284	145	-	2	1	71.00	75.73	1	-

	Inn	NO	Runs	HS	0s	50	100	Avrge	Stk/Rt	Ct	St
First Innings	33	2	1337	145	3	7	4	43.13	74.94	7	-
Second Innings	22	3	597	61	2	4	-	31.42	64.82	3	-

Venue	M	Inn	NO	Runs	HS	0s	50	100	Avrge	Stk/Rt	Ct	St
in Australia												
Adelaide	2	2	-	30	19	-	-	-	15.00	54.55	-	-
Brisbane	2	2	-	92	61	-	1	-	46.00	70.23	-	-
Melbourne	9	9	1	398	123	-	2	2	49.75	74.12	1	-
Perth	2	2	-	27	16	-	-	-	13.50	58.70	1	-
Sydney	7	7	-	324	84	1	3	-	46.29	72.81	3	-
in India												
Ahmedabad (SPS)	1	1	-	53	53	-	1	-	53.00	63.10	-	-
Chandigarh (MS)	1	1	-	0	0	1	-	-	0.00	0.00	-	-
Chennai (Corp)	1	1	-	31	31	-	-	-	31.00	72.09	-	-
Delhi (FSK)	2	2	-	186	145	-	-	1	93.00	89.00	-	-

Faridabad	1	-	17	17	-	-	17.00	60.71	-
Guwahati	1	-	0	0	1	-	0.00	0.00	-
Indore	1	-	35	35	-	-	35.00	68.63	-
Jaipur	1	-	102	102	-	1	102.00	90.27	-
Kanpur	1	-	84	84	-	1	84.00	70.59	-
Kochi	1	-	12	12	-	-	12.00	41.38	1
Mumbai (WS)	1	-	12	12	-	-	12.00	57.14	-
Nagpur	1	-	33	33	-	-	33.00	64.71	-
Visakhapatnam	1	-	6	6	-	-	6.00	42.86	1
in New Zealand									
Auckland	3	2	27	10*	-	-	27.00	67.50	1
Christchurch	1	1	10	10*	-	-	-	55.56	-
Dunedin	1	-	62	62	-	1	62.00	67.39	-
Napier	1	-	30	30	-	-	30.00	65.22	-
Wellington	2	-	27	26	-	-	13.50	75.00	-
in Pakistan									
Lahore	1	-	45	45	-	-	45.00	58.44	-
in Sri Lanka									
Colombo (PIS)	2	1	99	53	-	1	99.00	71.22	1
Colombo (SSC)	2	-	17	17	1	-	8.50	58.62	-
in United Arab Emirates									
Sharjah	4	-	132	52	-	1	33.00	80.49	1

in West Indies

	M	Inn	NO	Runs	HS	0s	50	100	Avrge	Stk/Rt	Ct	St
Georgetown	1	1	-	0	0	1	-	-	0.00	0.00	-	-
Port-of-Spain	1	1	-	43	43	-	-	-	43.00	63.24	-	-

Country	M	Inn	NO	Runs	HS	0s	50	100	Avrge	Stk/Rt	Ct	St
Australia	22	22	1	871	123	1	6	2	41.48	71.75	5	-
India	14	14	-	571	145	2	2	2	40.79	73.21	2	-
New Zealand	8	8	3	156	62	-	1	-	31.20	67.24	1	-
Pakistan	1	1	-	45	45	-	-	-	45.00	58.44	-	-
Sri Lanka	4	4	1	116	53	1	1	-	38.67	69.05	1	-
Sharjah	4	4	-	132	52	-	1	-	33.00	80.49	1	-
West Indies	2	2	-	43	43	1	-	-	21.50	61.43	-	-

Batting Position	Inn	NO	Runs	HS	0s	50	100	Avrge	Stk/Rt
3	40	1	1504	145	2	8	3	38.56	69.95
4	9	1	366	123	1	3	1	45.75	77.05
5	2	-	0	0	2	-	-	0.00	0.00
6	4	3	64	46*	-	-	-	64.00	83.12

Wickets: Ttl Bwd Cgt C&B LBW Stp HW
 - - - - - - -

Dismissals: Inns NO Bwd Cgt LBW Stp RO HW HB
 55   5   9   27   4   5   5   -   -

Highest Score: 145*   Australia v Zimbabwe, Delhi (FSK), 1997–98

100s	Team	Opponent	Venue	Season
123*	Australia	Sri Lanka	Melbourne	1995/96
102	Australia	West Indies	Jaipur	1995/96
100	Australia	New Zealand	Melbourne	1997/98
145	Australia	Zimbabwe	Delhi (FSK)	1997/98

Batting—Innings by Innings

Gme	Inn	Date	Team	Opp	Venue	Inn	Pos	HO	Fielder	Bowler	Runs	(Bls)	Ttl	Avrge	Stk/rt	Ct	St
1	1	15/02/1995	AUS	SAF	Wellington	2	6	BWD		EO Simons	1	(6)	1	1.00	16.67	-	-
2	2	19/02/1995	AJS	NZ	Auckland	1	6	NO			10*	(8)	11	11.00	78.57	-	-
3	3	22/02/1995	AUS	IND	Dunedin	1	3	CGT	PS Vaidya	M Prabhakar	62	(92)	73	36.50	68.87	-	-
4	4	26/02/1995	AUS	NZ	Auckland	2	6	NO			7*	(6)	80	40.00	71.43	-	-
5	5	12/03/1995	AUS	WI	Port-of-Spain	2	3	CGT	VC Drakes	PV Simmons	43	(68)	123	41.00	68.33	-	-
6	6	18/03/1995	AUS	WI	Georgetown	1	5	BWD		CL Hooper	0	(2)	123	30.75	67.58	-	-
7	7	17/12/1995	AUS	WI	Adelaide	1	4	STP	CO Browne	RA Harper	11	(21)	134	26.80	66.01	-	-
8	8	19/12/1995	AUS	WI	Melbourne	1	4	CGT	CO Browne	CA Walsh	6	(11)	140	23.33	65.42	1	-
9	9	21/12/1995	AUS	SL	Sydney	2	4	CGT	M Muralitharan	HDPK Dharmasena	56	(71)	196	28.00	68.77	-	-
10	10	01/01/1996	AUS	WI	Sydney	2	4	BWD		CEL Ambrose	0	(1)	196	24.50	68.53	-	-
11	11	07/01/1996	AUS	WI	Brisbane	2	4	CGT	RA Harper	IR Bishop	61	(86)	257	28.56	69.09	1	-
12	12	09/01/1996	AUS	SL	Melbourne	1	4	RO	(Kalpage/Kaluwitharana)		123	(142)	380	38.00	73.93	-	-
13	13	12/01/1996	AUS	SL	Perth	1	3	BWD		ST Jayasuriya	11	(19)	391	35.55	73.36	1	-
14	14	16/01/1996	AUS	SL	Melbourne	1	3	CGT	RS Kaluwitharana	GP Wickremsinghe	5	(12)	396	33.00	72.66	-	-
15	15	18/01/1996	AUS	SL	Melbourne	1	3	RO	(Mahanama)		51	(75)	447	34.38	72.10	-	-
16	16	20/01/1996	AJS	SL	Sydney	1	3	CGT	WPUJC Vaas	HDPK Dharmasena	17	(26)	464	33.14	71.83	-	-
17	17	23/02/1996	AUS	KYA	Visakhapatnam	1	3	CGT	K Otieno	R Ali	6	(14)	470	31.33	71.21	1	-
18	18	27/02/1996	AUS	IND	Mumbai (WS)	1	3	CGT	SV Manjrekar	SLV Raju	12	(21)	482	30.13	70.78	-	-
19	19	01/03/1995	AUS	ZIM	Nagpur	2	3	C&B	PA Strang	PA Strang	33	(51)	515	30.29	70.36	-	-

20	04/03/1996	AUS	WI	Jaipur	1	3	RO	(Ambrose/Harper)		102	(113)	617	34.28	73.02	-
21	11/03/1996	AUS	NZ	Chennai (Corp)	2	3	CGT	(S) RJ Kennedy	SA Thomson	31	(43)	648	34.11	72.97	-
22	14/03/1996	AUS	WI	Chandigarh (MS)	1	3	LBW		CEL Ambrose	0	(17)	648	32.40	71.60	-
23	17/03/1996	AUS	SL	Lahore	1	3	BWD		PA De Silva	45	(77)	693	33.00	70.57	-
24	26/08/1996	AUS	ZIM	Colombo (PIS)	1	3	C&B	GJ Whitall	GJ Whitall	53	(82)	746	33.91	70.11	1
25	30/08/1996	AUS	SL	Colombo (PIS)	1	6	NO			46*	(57)	792	36.00	70.65	-
26	06/09/1996	AUS	IND	Colombo (SSC)	2	3	LBW		SB Joshi	0	(3)	792	34.43	70.46	-
27	07/09/1996	AUS	SL	Colombo (SSC)	2	3	CGT	ST Jayasuriya	WPUJC Vaas	17	(26)	809	33.71	70.35	-
28	19/10/1996	AUS	SAF	Indore	1	3	CGT	DJ Richardson	AA Donald	35	(51)	844	33.76	70.27	-
29	25/10/1996	AUS	SAF	Faridabad	1	3	STP	DJ Richardson	PL Symcox	17	(28)	861	33.12	70.06	-
30	01/11/1996	AUS	SAF	Guwahati	1	5	BWD		N Boje	0	(1)	861	31.89	70.00	-
31	06/12/1996	AUS	WI	Melbourne	2	3	LBW		NAM McLean	5	(27)	866	30.93	68.89	-
32	08/12/1996	AUS	WI	Sydney	2	3	BWD		CA Walsh	44	(76)	910	31.38	68.27	-
33	15/12/1996	AUS	PAK	Adelaide	2	3	RO	(Waqar Younis)		19	(34)	929	30.97	67.96	-
34	09/12/1997	AUS	SAF	Melbourne	2	4	CGT	G Kirsten	L Klusener	15	(22)	944	30.45	67.96	-
35	17/12/1997	AUS	NZ	Melbourne	2	3	NO			60*	(92)	1004	32.39	67.79	-
36	11/01/1998	AUS	SAF	Brisbane	1	3	C&B	PL Symcox	PL Symcox	31	(45)	1035	32.34	67.82	-
37	14/01/1998	AUS	NZ	Sydney	1	4	BWD		CD McMillan	84	(103)	1119	33.91	68.69	1
38	18/01/1998	AUS	SAF	Perth	1	3	CGT	JH Kallis	PL Symcox	16	(27)	1135	33.38	68.54	-
39	21/01/1998	AUS	NZ	Melbourne	1	3	CGT	SB O'Connor	CL Cairns	100	(114)	1235	35.29	69.77	1
40	23/01/1998	AUS	SAF	Melbourne	2	3	CGT	DJ Richardson	AA Donald	33	(42)	1268	35.22	69.98	-
41	26/01/1998	AUS	SAF	Sydney	2	3	LBW		L Klusener	47	(72)	1315	35.54	69.80	-
42	27/01/1998	AUS	SAF	Sydney	1	3	STP	DJ Richardson	PR Adams	76	(96)	1391	36.61	70.25	1
43	08/02/1998	AUS	SAF	Christchurch	2	4	NO			10*	(18)	1401	36.87	70.12	-
44	10/02/1998	AUS	NZ	Wellington	1	3	CGT	SP Fleming	DJ Nash	26	(30)	1427	36.59	70.36	-
45	12/02/1998	AUS	NZ	Napier	1	3	CGT	SP Fleming	CZ Harris	30	(46)	1457	36.43	70.25	-
46	14/02/1998	AUS	NZ	Auckland	2	3	BWD		SB Doull	10	(26)	1467	35.78	69.86	1
47	01/04/1998	AUS	IND	Kochi	2	3	CGT	M Azharuddin	HH Kanitkar	12	(29)	1479	35.21	69.47	1
48	03/04/1998	AUS	ZIM	Ahmedabad (SPS)	1	3	RO	(A Flower-Viljoen)		53	(84)	1532	35.63	69.23	-

49	49	07/04/1998	AUS	IND	Kanpur	1	3	CGT	HH Kanitkar	AB Agarkar	84	(119)	1616	36.73	69.30	-
50	50	11/04/1998	AUS	ZIM	Delhi (FSK)	1	3	CGT	M Mbangwa	GJ Whittall	145	(158)	1761	39.13	70.72	-
51	51	14/04/1998	AUS	IND	Delhi (FSK)	2	3	STP	NR Mongia	R Sanghvi	41	(51)	1802	39.17	70.92	-
52	52	18/04/1998	AUS	NZ	Sharjah	2	3	CGT	MJ Horne	CZ Harris	52	(71)	1854	39.45	70.98	-
53	53	19/04/1998	AUS	IND	Sharjah	1	3	CGT	AR Kumble	HH Kanitkar	48	(65)	1902	39.63	71.05	1
54	54	22/04/1998	AUS	IND	Sharjah	1	3	STP	NR Mongia	Singh Harbhajan	31	(26)	1933	39.45	71.51	-
55	55	24/04/1998	AUS	IND	Sharjah	1	3	CGT	NR Mongia	VBK Prasad	1	(2)	1934	38.68	71.50	-